PAY THE PRICE

Creating Ethical Entrepreneurial Success Through Passion, Pain and Purpose

BY STEVEN N. ADJEI

Publishing Services provided by Paper Raven Books LLC

Printed in the United States of America

First Printing, 2022

Paperback ISBN: 978-1-7396211-0-0

Hardback ISBN: 978-1-7396211-1-7

PRAISE FOR PAY THE PRICE

"In the 2020s, Pay The Price *is a very timely, well-written book that keeps our attention, feels essential, and is a lovely read. This is such a refreshing and realistic antidote to the fantasy that in business everything is easy, and success is deserved and inevitable. Highly recommended."*

-**Charlie Roberston** - Global Chief Economist and Head of Macro Strategy at Renaissance Capital and author of the bestselling books The Fastest Billion and The Time-Traveling Economist

Charlie is the first ever non-African winner of the African Banker Icon Award for his pioneering work in transforming the financial sector in Africa. He has also been voted the #1 frontier analyst for 5 consecutive years by Thomson Reuters Extel from 2016-2020.

"Finally, a business book with soul about the businesses that actually make the world go round—small and medium enterprises. This is not just a must-read for any practicing or aspiring entrepreneurs or intrapreneurs—it is a must-read for anyone who is trying to find the golden thread that makes their life make sense. A tapestry of deep contextual experience, raw vulnerability, and great storytelling based on insights drawn from an eclectic range of fields makes for a compelling and entertaining read regardless of your professional or social background. Deeply satisfying like a bag of treats you can't stop eating that leaves you craving more."

-**Dr. Ernest Darkoh-Ampem** - Founding Partner, BroadReach Corporation.

Ernest has more than 25 years of experience developing and implementing innovative health interventions at scale. He has been named one of Time *magazine's 18 Global Health Heroes and New Africa's 100 Most Influential Africans, and has served on President Obama's Presidential Advisory Council on HIV/AIDS. He is a Fulbright Scholar from Oxford's Saïd Business School, and holds Medical and Public Health degrees from Harvard.*

"It is my pleasure and honour to enthusiastically recommend Pay the Price. *This pioneering book lays out the entrepreneurial challenges of serving humanity through compassion, courage and gratitude. A compelling and refreshing read."*

- **Robert Smith** - Founder, Conscious Capital, Switzerland.

Robert is an advisor to the Permanent Secretariat of the World Summit of Nobel Peace Laureates and has been recognised as one of the world's top 100 Visionary leaders by the Real Leaders Magazine *and also holds various board positions at the UN Capital Development Fund and The Harmon Foundation.*

"In Pay The Price, *Steven Adjei shows that honesty, accountability and care for others is always worth the cost. Steven encourages each of us to understand our deepest roots—even our pain and bad habits—and to seek growth. When we do, with the help of others, we can push away obstacles and set our hearts and minds on leaving a legacy that lasts."*

- **Sam Black** - Director of Recovery Education, Covenant Eyes, Michigan, United States

Formerly Vice President of Business Development at Covenant Eyes, Sam is an author and world-renowned specialist in helping people break addictions.

"What a great book! Very few books offer a truly new perspective, but Pay The Price *is certainly one of them. Love the stories from Africa. Love the way he frames them. Love the pain and passion that shines through. A powerful voice that needs to be heard."*

- **Professor Christian Stadler** - Professor of Strategic Management at Warwick Business School and best-selling author of *Open Strategy*, 2021 Business Strategy Book of the Year.

Christian is listed as a future thinker by Thinkers50, the premier ranking of the most influential thinkers of the world, and also the bestselling author of Enduring Success. He has written for the New York Times, Wall Street Journal, *and has a regular blog on* Forbes *magazine.*

"*Steven's combination of utter humility, but outstanding intelligence is breathtaking. The range of references, ideas and inspirations in this book will blow your mind. Pay the Price is absolutely what Steven did to collect this wisdom, an author who has done the hard yards and lets us share every bit of wisdom he gained along the way. If you want to feel immediately inspired to expand your own ambitions and ways of looking at the world, read this book!*"

- **Anderson Hirst** - CEO, Selling Interactions, and founding partner, Kojo Academy

Anderson is a world-renowned sales management expert who has dedicated his career to sales excellence, working with a range of clients including Volvo, Novartis, Oracle, Warwick Business School, Leo Pharma, and Skoda.

"*In* Pay The Price, *Steven intentionally shows the true scars of entrepreneurship. Rejecting the typical business book approach of the magic success formula or even the dramatic shaming of the falling villain, Steven offers a human, and at times raw, account of the journey that anyone takes in building a business. Often when I read business books, I feel excited or stimulated with ideas, and like a sugar rush, that sensation soon passes. Not this time. Rarely do I feel such a deep resonance and connection as I have with* Pay The Price—*a book of vulnerability, wisdom, passion, hope and pragmatism.*"

- **Claire Oatway** - Executive Leadership Coach, keynote speaker, and CEO of Neon Juno

Claire is a 2021 World Top Ten Executive Coach according to influencive.com, a luminary speaker, and an expert in the intersection between AI and Ethics.

"*In addition to fresh, compelling, and intriguing perspectives on Pain, Ethics and Legacy,* Pay the Price *offers a rare and important window into the promising world of emerging entrepreneurship, where the future of impact investing inevitably lies. Highly recommended.*"

- **Les Funtleyder** – Professor at Columbia University and bestselling author of *Healthcare Investing*

Les is an internationally recognized expert on healthcare investing, a frequent pundit on CNBC and Bloomberg, and a Professor at the Mailman School of Public Health at Columbia University and a multi-million dollar healthcare investor.

"In Pay The Price, *Steven takes the reader on a creative, rock-and-roll journey into ethical entrepreneurship, and what happens when great African minds solve real problems with practical sustainable solutions. The time and opportunity to transition from donor funding to marketplaces is here, and Steven creates a powerful picture inspiring hopefully many entrepreneurs to do the same."*

  - **Nicole Spieker** - CEO PharmAccess Foundation, Amsterdam, Netherlands

    For 20 years, PharmAccess has been one of the leading organisations that has worked to make inclusive health markets work in sub-Saharan Africa. PharmAccess facilitates loans to healthcare entrepreneurs as well as innovative value-based healthcare solutions, financing, and data.

"In Pay The Price, *Steven has portrayed the courage and determination required for anyone wanting to embark on the path of entrepreneurship. The book highlights the importance of motivation, integrity, and ambition, which are the pillars of all great journeys, and shows that when these foundations are strong, success is unbounded. Thoroughly enjoyed reading it and very highly recommended!"*

  - **Avni Patel** – MRPharmS, Director, The Wellcare Group, United Kingdom

    Avni is one of the UK's most exciting young pharma female entrepreneurs and was pivotal in delivering vaccines during the COVID pandemic in London and the South West of England and has been recognised by the BBC for her work in this regard.

"Steven N. Adjei should be commended for his candor and showing such vulnerability in Pay The Price. *By sharing so openly his own challenges and successes, he gives aspiring entrepreneurs a good sense of what to expect. He also provides each of us food for thought on values and ethical entrepreneurship."*

  - **Professor Elikem Kuenyehia** – Professor of Practice at Buckingham University, bestselling author and *Art Aficionado.*

    Elikem is a Professor of Practice at Buckingham University in the United Kingdom, a thought leader and author on entrepreneurship, and the founder of the Kuenyehia Prize for African Contemporary Art, one of Africa's most prestigious Contemporary Art Awards.

TABLE OF CONTENTS

THE INTRO

THE HONEYMOON PERIOD   25

THE FORMATIVE PERIOD   77

THE LEGACY PERIOD   203

THE OUTRO

ACCESS THE SPOTIFY PLAYLIST

Scan the QR code to listen to
the *Pay the Price* Spotify playlist!

FREE GIFT

Visit **www.stevenadjei.com** to sign up and receive
a FREE book of Steven's poetry,
African award-winning art, and much more!

DEDICATION

To my only daughter, Nshira;

A knack for business.
A heart for the world.
A love for people.

You represent the future of Ethical Entrepreneurship.

I am, and always will be a proud, proud father, and I love you more than words can say. I hope this book does you and your generation the justice you deserve to make the world a better place after we, 'the oldies,' have almost ruined it.

To my only and late sister, Glenda Jane.

Your joy for life and your love for people lifted everyone around you.
Your sudden passing shocked me, both in a bad way, but sowed the seeds for my business.
And this book.

You represented the best in mankind. Unconditional love.

Rest in peace.

FOREWORD

The message at the heart of this book is 'Follow Your Dreams.' Reality dictates that a few nightmares have to be faced along the way. What makes this book so life-affirming is its recognition that it is essential for the individual to preserve their inner core of personal integrity whilst doing so.

By the end of this book you will know Steven Adjei well. It reflects the person I have come to know and admire, who embodies the principles of ethical entrepreneurism and fairness which he espouses in this volume. Honesty, too—this is an imperfect human being who has suffered some serious health issues and made some bad personal and business decisions, but who has built on those experiences to come to an understanding of what he describes as WGLL: What Good Looks Like.

The volume is primarily aimed at business students and aspiring entrepreneurs (however you choose to define entrepreneurship), and there are certainly important lessons for—and questions addressed to—them. But this is no ordinary textbook (and I am no entrepreneur!); it casts its net wide across the arts and sciences, into stories and poetry and of course music. Steven's aspiration for the readers of *Pay The Price*, for entrepreneurs and non-entrepreneurs alike, is that they might have better prospects of success once they have absorbed the lessons here.

That seems to me to be entirely plausible—and in the process they will have come to know themselves better as the result of Steven taking the courageous decision to share this absorbing journey.

Happy reading!
Professor Sir Myles A Wickstead
Bath, England
July 2022

PROLOGUE—HOLDING MY BREATH

Holding My Breath

At the shrine of hopelessness
I lay my wreath.
Adorned with flowers, weeds, roses and thorns
Woven inexplicably
Woven inextricably
With fears, tears, blood and sweat.

Looking upwards
I lift my gaze
Through the maze
Of life.

And wonder why
I keep holding my breath
Laying my wreath…
…and waiting.

- Steven N. Adjei, *Excerpt from* From Gory to Glory: The Sorry Details

FIRST WORD

Saturday, 17 July, 2021.

We all sometimes need a jolt in life to get us moving in the right direction.
Not surprisingly, I needed multiple jolts. Dela, my wife, calls me the king
of procrastination. I have mastered the art to perfection.

I needed multiple jolts. And I got them last week.

I had been harbouring this book somewhere in my mind's womb (and
in multiple journals) for at least two years. I had annotated the points to
death but had not actually started. I bought a manual on how to write
a book, a couple of journals, nice pens, books on entrepreneurship, and
even purchased a brand-new Mac. But there was nothing on paper.

The first jolt was a literal jolt. It came in the form of a huge crash.

I lay at the bottom of the stairs, a vacuum cleaner in my hand, unconscious.
As I came to, my family was all around me. My daughter was wailing
in fear and distress; my wife was trying to help me to my feet; my son
was somewhere upstairs running around like a maniac. I had left a trail
of destruction—fractured furniture, destroyed decorations, a ransacked
radiator, gory, bleeding gashes to my back and arms, and, possibly most
of all, punctured pride.

I was knocked out cold. Contorted on the ground, foaming, helpless, and rigid.

I had had an epileptic fit at the top of the stairs whilst trying to do some housework with a 20kg Shark vacuum cleaner in my hand. This was the third time this disease had almost killed me. The first was at a roundabout at Derry's Cross, Plymouth City Centre in 2012, when I was leaving the gym and driving to a consultancy project job at Mevagissey, Cornwall in England. I had a fit, crashed my brand-new pride and joy, and nearly ran over a taxi driver.

The second was at Plymstock, Devon, four years later when I had another fit and crashed our family Volkswagen Golf on my way to the post office to pick up a parcel. I was fortunate to walk out alive, seeing the state of both cars that had to be written off due to the impact of the accident.

And the second jolt? A phone call from Professor Sir Myles Wickstead, KCMG CBE. Professor Wickstead was a mentor to me for over half a decade. He was recently knighted by Her Majesty the Queen in June 2021 in recognition of his exceptional and sustained contribution to international development, in roles too numerous to mention here. He was also a bestselling author, professor at two of the UK's most prestigious universities—King's College, London and University of Exeter—and a trustee of the BBC Media Action. He has dedicated the last 15 years of his life to helping the world's poorest people in countless roles.

It so happened that I was thinking of someone who knew me personally, had been involved with my journey right from the beginning, and who fit the ticket of an ethical and just a plain brilliant human being, known the world over. He fit the ticket, rang at just the right time, and was excited when I mentioned the book. More excited than I was.

And finally, the third jolt: my genius 15-year-old daughter had just won the National Enterprise Award for the most enterprising student in a key stage group in the UK. She was chosen from thousands of entries across the country after a brilliant idea, an advertisement, and an interview.

As I came round, bleeding from the deep gashes on my back and arms, surrounded by chaos both internally and externally, it suddenly came to me.

The Eureka moment.

In a split second I realized this fall down the stairs had epitomised my business struggles over the previous decade.

Being at the top, falling down, ending up on the ground—wounded, scarred, limping, but with the courage to get up and start again. As I climbed back up the stairs to have a shower and get my wounds dressed, I looked down and saw the trail of destruction the fall had left—the legacy of the fit.

What kind of legacy did I want to leave?

Hopefully, a final happy ending after the 10-year struggle with dragons of all types: the fiery kind with the pitchfork, the imaginary kind in my head, and the humankind, named and unnamed. Yes, human beings could be dragons too.

They had not been kind, but my price had been paid. Success beckoned. It had a date and a name: Saturday, 17 July, 2021. Pay the Price. The day I finally started writing this book and the day I signed my first million-dollar deal.

PREFACE

"Entrepreneurship is the most sure way of development."
-Paul Kagame, Current President of Rwanda

Entrepreneurship.

Courses and modules have been taught in leading business schools, and hundreds of books have been written on the subject. I have read scores of them myself. (By the way, a lot of the literature and books out there are fantastic, and the latest one I am reading, *How I Built This* by Guy Raz, I found inspiring.)

But the truth is that many of them fail. And starting a business is a lot, lot harder than most people think.

Research done in 2019 showed that 90% of US businesses had failed by the 10th year. The trend is similar in the UK, with 60 percent failing in their 3rd year and 90 percent failing by the 10th year.

The 10th year seems to be significant, for reasons which will be explored further on in this book.

Failure rates are worse in developing countries due to obvious harsher economic headwinds. According to the Better Africa report, 75 percent of businesses in Ethiopia, Ghana, Rwanda, and Nigeria, and around 60 percent in Kenya, South Africa, and Nigeria, shut down in just the first year. Even the traditional reasons for staying in paid 9-to-5 employment—security, dependability, and a guaranteed paycheck each month—are waning.

In a very recent (March 2022) *Harvard Business Review* article titled "Workers Don't Feel Like a 9-to-5 Job Is a Safe Bet Anymore," Carolyn Ockels, Steve King, and Gene Zaino state:

> Job security is a key reason people choose traditional employment over traditional work. But declining perceptions of job security, coupled with workers rethinking what they want when it comes to work/life balance, are leading more people to prioritise flexibility, autonomy, and control when choosing where they will work. New data shows that the percentage of traditional full-time workers who believe independent work is more secure than traditional work has increased significantly in the last four years.[1]

But these bleak statistics don't deter people from trying. There is something deep in our psyche that moves us to explore, to try, and to reach, even though the odds of failure are deep.

There is no shortage of literature that tries to explain these failure rates. For example, running out of cash, no market need, team differences, and competition and pricing/cost issues are frequently mentioned. While there is certainly some truth to these analyses, a lot of the literature tends to fall prey to what Phil Rosenzweig calls the halo effect. His book of the same name offers a critique of the way that many treatments of entrepreneurship fall prey to "pseudo-science, which operates at the level of storytelling, but has a façade of 'superficial trappings of science.'" In what follows, I will attempt to account for the rates of failure mentioned above without falling prey to the halo effect. First, however, a bit more about the halo effect itself.

John Kay, writing in the *Financial Times* on 7 May, 2007, describes the halo effect:

> The power of the halo effect means that when things are going well, praise spills over to every aspect of performance, but also that when the wheel of fortune spins, the reappraisal is equally extensive. Our search for excessively simple

---

1 *Workers Don't Feel Like a 9-to-5 Job Is a Safe Bet Anymore* by Ockels, King, Zaino, HBR, 23 March 2022

explanations, our desire to find great men and excellent companies, gets in the way of the complex truth.

Phil Rosenzweig uses Jim Collins's runaway bestselling book, *Good to Great,* as an example of how using flawed data may lead to flawed results:

> Here's a brutal fact we may wish to consider: If you start by selecting companies based on outcome, and then gather data by conducting retrospective interviews and from the business press, you're not likely to discover what led some companies to become Great. You'll mainly catch the glow from the Halo Effect.

This was a brave statement from Rosenweig.

The book *Good to Great* was the result of five years of intensive research, 15,000 hours, dozens of books, 6,000 articles, and scores of interviews. It churned out data that was equivalent to 384 million bytes and filled many crates and entire cabinets, certainly a scientific approach. But Phil Rosenzweig was not impressed: "The quality of the data is what's important, not the quantity," he says.

15 years on, we still appear to be making the same mistake. A typical example is Netflix. Reid Hoffman, along with respected publications like *The Economist,* praised Netflix profusely several years ago, when things were going well. Now that Netflix is currently the worst-performing stock in the S&P 500 index, and was worth 40 percent less on April 19th, 2022 than the very next day, April 20th, major publications are now lining up to discredit its business model. *The Guardian,* for instance, says it has become "fat and dull, with an outsized appetite for increasingly low-calorie content—the very thing it once disdained—just another expensive TV package."

Regarding the leadership of Reed Hastings, *Bloomberg* says, "Reed Hastings has led the company for more than two decades and has earned the respect of shareholders—but if Netflix continues to shed customers—the board—or an investor, may agitate for a change." Reed himself appeared "unconcerned about competition" in 2018, but now acknowledges that

"Alphabet, Amazon, and Meta are tremendously powerful, so there's not easy money there" according to *The Economist* article.

But the truth is, not many of us will ever reach these dizzying heights of success. Nor should all of us aspire to. There is nothing wrong with being content as a small business owner.

Most of what I have read also tends to concentrate on the big successes— Airbnb, Dyson, LinkedIn, Google, Apple, Amazon, Facebook, and Bumble to name a few.

But the truth is 99 percent of the economies of the world are dependent on small- and medium-size enterprises (SMEs) and yet, there is scarce literature devoted to lessons they can teach us. I mention a few in this book, and I have been incredibly inspired by their stories. Most business authors, books, consultancies, and companies pay lip service to these incredible companies, but at the end, all "*bow down to the altar of Apple et. al*" as SME business consultant Nick Shuff points out.

In fact, I have come across only two books that took a stab at exploring this topic. These books are *The Roadside MBA* by Michael Mazzeo, Paul Oyer, and Scott Schaeffer, and the bestseller *The E-Myth* by Michael Gerber.

So why do so many fail?

As I mentioned above, this book has been written to explore the topic without falling prey to the halo effect. Even more specifically and importantly, the reason why I wrote this book is to encourage entrepreneurs while giving them a sense of what to really expect when they start their businesses. The more entrepreneurs know about the difficulties that might lie ahead, the more stability and longevity they are likely to have.

And businesses do need to be started. Entrepreneurs are vital, necessary, crucial even. The problems in this world that need solving are steadily increasing. And more than ever, these problems need solving at a local level.

It is my firm belief that free enterprise, and the curiosity and ingenuity that sustain it, has the capacity to solve these problems. However, in order to meet the ever-changing problems of the world, we have to start looking at entrepreneurship through a different lens.

QUESTIONS:

1. Where have you noticed the halo effect, in news or in your own work?

ETHICAL ENTREPRENEURSHIP

I think I can hear a yawn. Not another book on solving problems, profit with purpose, or saving the planet. Or for that matter, a book on the policies of free market enterprise and the importance of competition. By ethical entrepreneurship, I mean something completely different. Different, even, than the concept of social entrepreneurship that is in vogue now.

The notion of ethical entrepreneurship is not so much about the idea, or the reason, or the business, crucial though they are, but *the person.*

The ethical entrepreneur has good business practices, a love for humanity, and a desire to see a better world deeply ingrained in her psyche. It informs every decision, every step, every dream. It comes from within and radiates without. And in this way, the ethical entrepreneur is the same person everywhere.

This, of course, doesn't mean she doesn't make stupid mistakes, or turn onto the wrong road from time to time, but it means that the inner compass keeps redirecting her to true north, time and time again. And this continual struggle, this battle, lasts forever. It's a battle that gets more ferocious with time, right to the end.

When writing this book, I had to seek inspiration beyond traditional sources to convey my vision of ethical entrepreneurship. You may notice as you read that in addition to literature on entrepreneurship, I have also relied heavily on personal experiences, as well as poetry and music. You will find references to lots of bands, poets, and musicians from every genre littered throughout the book. They have been my mainstay and inspiration. And you likely will never have heard of them.

But that's the point, as we will see later in this chapter.

So, why do most entrepreneurial ventures fail, and where could they succeed? To answer that question, I will explore several principles that undergird entrepreneurial success:

- Start With Who
- The Definition of Success
- The Importance of Scalability
- The Pain and Process of the Formative Period

START WITH WHO

If you
Were married to yourself
Could you stay with yourself?
My house
Would be frightening and wild.

- Yrsa Daley-Ward, "Q," *Bone*, 2017

In 2009, Simon Sinek launched a TED Talk called "Start With Why." It became a hugely influential lecture on the TED network and is currently ranked as the third most-watched TED Talk of all time.

This talk spun the bestselling book in 2011 of the same name. In the book, Sinek argues that there is something you'll find in every great leader and successful organisation—a sense of purpose. Sinek contends that people do their best work when they know why they're doing what they're doing. He argues that success is the fruit of design, not of short-term patches.

However, this book argues that while we may start by looking for a sense of purpose—a why—the why ultimately flows from the who. In other words, why I do what I do has its basis in who I am as a person. A bad apple tree can never produce good apples, no matter the soil, the climate, the gardener, or the fertiliser.

So, the focus of this book will not only be on the purpose, but on the person. Because a good, ethically motivated entrepreneur will always strive to build a good, ethically motivated business, no matter what field they happen to engage.

Because sometimes, we forget the blindingly obvious.

The entrepreneur is a person. An ordinary, living, breathing person with fears, hopes, and dreams just like every one of us. We all succumb to the same ethical laws and principles of life. And ethical principles, as famous author and leadership coach John Maxwell says, are irrefutable. They are just there. You can bump against them, try to circumvent them, hit your head against them, or bring a wrecking ball to try to break them down, but they are just what they are—immovable, irrefutable, eternal. And they govern our lives, whether we like it or not. And trying to ignore them is as useless as chasing after the wind.

QUESTIONS:

1. Take some time to reflect on the orientation and values that drive you in business and more broadly as a person. How would you describe them?

2. How have these values informed your entrepreneurial journey thus far? How could they do so more fully?

THE DEFINITION OF SUCCESS

I got dreams that keep up me up in the dead of night
Telling me I wasn't made for the simple life
There's a light I see, but it's far in the distance
I'm asking you to show me some forgiveness
It's all for you in my pursuit of happiness.

- NEEDTOBREATHE, "Happiness," *H A R D L O V E*, 2015

To be successful, we focus on the market need, the business case, raising the money, and keeping the lights on. These are all crucial. But it's the doggedness, the resilience—in short, the spirit of "get rich or die trying," as 50 Cent said—that enables many to beat the odds. These traits, illuminated by reasoned enlightenment, validation, common sense, and, most importantly, contribution to the betterment of mankind, create the foundation for real and lasting success.

In the light of this, success also needs to be understood beyond simple metrics such as financial performance. In fact, at the risk of over-quoting *The Halo Effect,* Phil Rosenweig makes this same point:

> What's the most relevant and tangible information we often have about a company? Financial performance, of course. Whether the company is profitable. Whether sales are growing. Whether the price of its stock is on the rise. Financial performance looks to be accurate and objective. Numbers don't lie, as we like to say—which is why Enron, Tyco, and a handful of other recent scandals shake our confidence so deeply. We routinely trust financial performance figures. And it's natural that on the basis of this performance data, people make attributions on other things that are less tangible and objective.

This statement is still true, even now. Most of us would have heard about the recent scandal of WeWork, popularised by the 2021 book *The Cult of We* by Eliot Brown and Maureen Farrell, and by the 2022 series on Apple

TV—*WeCrashed*. And how the most prominent investors in the world were blinded to the company's glaring risks for nearly a decade.

Real success requires both financial metrics, **and** a higher purpose, and here, ethical entrepreneurship has a vital role:

Pan-African businessman and billionaire telecom entrepreneur Strive Masiyiwa, founder of Econet Global and Cassava Technologies, and the African Union's Special Envoy in the fight against COVID, writes:

> At the beginning of the COVID pandemic in 2020, I was told that one of the biggest problems was testing for the virus.
>
> African countries had no access to test kits and masks (used in hospitals). We have probably already forgotten how hard it was to get them. But it was not that long ago that African governments were paying crazy prices for these things. Corruption erupted across the continent, as unscrupulous thieves moved in to take advantage. Some ministers and civil servants even joined in!
>
> I was asked by President Cyril Ramaphosa to solve the problem.
>
> The first thing I did was to study the problem to understand why it was happening. It became clear that there were not enough of the test kits and masks being produced, and suppliers were demanding large volume orders beyond what most African countries could produce on their own.
>
> "Why can't we buy together?" I asked.
>
> "How can 55 countries buy together? How do you coordinate the orders and payments?" someone else asked.
>
> I went away to think about it. I remembered how shared economy models worked for businesses like Amazon, eBay, and Jumia.

"What if we build a website and ask countries to place their orders there, and then we ask suppliers to display their goods, if they want big orders? Let me find someone who understands how these platforms are designed and how they work. Someone with experience in e-commerce fulfilment."

I knew just the person: Ms. Fatoumata Ba of Senegal. Fatoumata said she would do it as a volunteer, but I would need to pay her team. I gave her some of my own people from Vaya Africa to work with.

They mobilized over 30 experts to start working on the platform.

Next: "What about payments? Suppliers want to be paid upfront, and we will need hundreds of millions of dollars."

My reply: "Let's talk to a bank that understands bulk trade and see what they think." And with that I called Professor Benedict Oramah of the African Export Import Bank (better known as AfriEximbank).

"If you build the platform, we will provide the financing to support bulk purchasing by our member states," the professor stated. And he immediately put up people and money to support the development.

"How do we recruit countries to use the platform?" I asked him.

"Talk to Vera. She is the one who knows all the Finance Ministers. Also, John will bring the Health Ministers." Vera is the highly respected Dr. Vera Songwe, who heads the United Nations Economic Commission for Africa. John is Dr. John Nkengasong, the Head of the Africa CDC.

The four of us became known as "the principals" by our staff. We met every day, just like entrepreneurs starting a new business!

Within six weeks we had built the Africa Medical Supplies Platform: www. AMSP.Africa.

I presented it (pitched it) to the 10 African heads of State who were the leadership executives last year, known as the Bureau of Presidents.

I took them through the website and asked them to try it. They were so happy: "You have solved our problem!" they all said. The next day President Ramaphosa, as Chair of the African Union at the time, called a Press Conference and presented it to the world.

Suppliers began to list their products, and countries began to buy. Prices came down dramatically. Soon, they wanted us to expand the range of products beyond COVID-related products. I got a call from President Kenyatta, and he asked me if it would be okay for the Caribbean countries to join. We immediately invited them, and 14 member-states, led by Jamaica, registered on the platform.

AMSP is registered as a not-for-profit business. All its profits (2.5 percent commission on all sales) are directed to the Africa Centres for Disease Control (CDC), which helps us monitor and fight pandemics.[2]

Not every problem out there is screaming for a political solution. Leaders need to trust those with the right skills to step forward and help them.

Today, the AMSP is the largest e-commerce platform in Africa by volume of products sold and by value. This is ethical entrepreneurship in pictures. You absolutely can make money **AND** make an impact through entrepreneurship. And that should be your goal. Your ethos. Possessions with purpose.

In his bestselling book, *Impact: Reshaping Capitalism to Drive Real Change,* Sir Ronald Cohen observes:

> All over the world, capitalism and democracy are being forcefully challenged. It is becoming increasingly clear that current levels of inequality are unsustainable, and many people around the world, in both developed and emerging countries, are rebelling against the unfair distribution of social economic and environmental outcomes.

---

2 https://www.ifc.org/wps/wcm/connect/news_ext_content/ifc_external_corporate_site/news+and+events/
news/insights/africa-recovery

He continues:

> Yet, unaided, governments and philanthropists cannot be expected to bring the urgently needed solutions, and governments are waking up to the fact that they are not always best placed to provide the innovative solutions we need.

From here, Cohen talks about the advent of impact investing, and whilst I agree in principle, investing in the right kind of entrepreneurial business and entrepreneur is crucial if it is to fuel innovative businesses that will drive a world economy "able to use free markets to grow, but to also help those whom rising prosperity has left stranded."[3]

Impact trumps mere financial success every time.

Mrs. Bernice Atubra is the proprietor of Henry House International School, a pre-university college in Ho, Ghana. She comes from a lineage of educationalists. Her father was one of the top educationists in Ghana after whom the school was named. The conviction to start Henry House came to her in a dream, and was reinforced later when two children were presented to her who had just finished school but could hardly read or write.

She vowed that she would start a high-quality school that would provide a well-rounded education to students in one of the most impoverished regions in Southern Ghana. This was not to be a social enterprise—she envisioned it as a full-fledged business. To realize her vision, she moved to Ghana from the UK with her husband and invested her savings, pension, and donations into the school. They sold their $500,000.00 house, her husband gave up his lucrative job as a gynaecologist, and they made the jump.

Ten years later, the school had not been completed and was still not financially stable. Her husband developed severe dementia, and they ran into severe financial problems. Eventually, they had to return to the UK, licking their wounds. They rented a two-bedroom flat where Bernice is

---

3 Cohen Ronald. Impact: Reshaping Capitalism to Drive Real Change (London, Random House, 2020)

now stuck indoors twenty-four hours a day nursing her sick husband. Savings, pension, investment all gone.

She has endured mass ridicule, been left depressed, full of tears daily, and her husband of over 30 years can barely speak. Has she failed? Or has she succeeded?

Look closer and the impact of her decision begins to show. The school, built in a rural poor part of western Ghana, has won accolades nationwide for the quality of its education, such as the country's coveted National Spelling Bee award, beating much more established schools built in more prosperous parts of the country. It's educated hundreds of students, many of whom are now leaders in their fields, and provided steady employment for scores of teachers and auxiliary workers.

Wayne Berry was an entrepreneur who grew up on a council estate in Warrington, Manchester. He grew up as a troubled kid, witnessing abuse which many of us could not even imagine and losing his dad in his teens which sent him into an angry spiral, culminating in a pub brawl which nearly got him into jail. Most people had already written him off.

But that experience of narrowly avoiding jail shook him. He got himself together, skilled up, matured, achieved, and doors began to open. But the unfairness of business reared its head, not least because of his upbringing and origins. He got undervalued, passed up for promotion and disrespected. Again.

At 30, he'd had enough, went down the entrepreneurial route, and Jaw Digital was born. He built the business from nothing. Growing rapidly, it soon began to win awards and scale.

After five years, Wayne was suddenly successful. The trappings beckoned. The holidays. Nice house. Shopping.

Then COVID struck. Then a massive flood destroyed the office. All the sectors he worked for, dental and hair transplants, were the first to go under. He also had two children born during COVID. He tried to rescue the business, but at the end of May 2022, Jaw Digital had to be liquidated. Wayne was devastated, exhausted, and drained. Talk about multiplied bad luck.

But out of this, a new passion was born. When I spoke to him on a recent conference call, I was struck by his realism, lessons he had learned, and most of all, a new desire to build a brand-new, ethical business that would focus on 'giving back.'

Out of this, a new podcast was born.

Chav in the Boardroom, he called it, a podcast dedicated to inspire people like him—underprivileged, poor, downbeat youngsters to make something out of their lives. He's already interviewed famous celebrities from the same deprived area as he: George Sampson, former *Britain's Got Talent* winner.

I came away from that conference call with a new friend and a new inspiration. Once again, just like in Bernice's case, failure had ignited success. But a different kind of success. A success founded not only on financial reward, but on legacy impact for underprivileged kids.

So, even in the midst of financial failure, seeds of success are everywhere to be seen.[4]

QUESTIONS:

1. Can you think of examples—whether from your own life or from elsewhere—of success that involve sacrifice?

2. Does Bernice's story reveal any preconceptions you might have about what success looks like?

3. What does Wayne's story mean to you as an aspiring ethical entrepreneur?

---

4 A percentage of proceeds from the sale of this book will be donated to completing the building and expanding Bernice's vision.

THE IMPORTANCE OF SCALABILITY

'Cause we're gonna be legends
Gonna get their attention
What we're doing here ain't just scary
It's about to be legendary

Yeah, we're gonna be legends
Teach 'em all a lesson
Got this feeling in our souls we carry
It's about to be legendary…

- Welshly Arms, "Legendary," *Legendary*, 2019

The idea of scalability came to me from the most unlikely source: movies and television. For about a month, I happened to be watching the show *The Blacklist* and the popular medical series *The Resident*, as well as the movie *Den of Thieves*. As an avid lover of rock music, I noticed two songs I'd heard when watching other movies and television shows. Still, I didn't know who the artists were.

Thank goodness for Shazam, a godsend app.

I realised that the songs were called "Legendary" and "Sanctuary," by a band I had never heard of: Welshly Arms. A quick check on Spotify revealed their songs. Motivational, almost soulful, they have now become a mainstay of my morning run—and of many mainstream movies.

The Blacklist has won multiple Emmy Awards, the latest being in 2020. It won the Screen Actors Guild Award in 2016. It is now one of the most popular television series in the US and the UK.

Den of Thieves was nominated for the National Film and Television Awards in 2018 in the US.

Lucifer has also been nominated for Emmy Awards (2021) and won numerous other awards. But Welshly Arms has not won a single music award and has just over a million listeners on Spotify. The scalability of their songs has brought them success. Even though they are hardly well known as a band.

The importance of scalability also means that the ethical entrepreneur may have to accept that the foundations of their business model limits how far they can realistically go, physically, at least. Also, they may have to embrace the possibility that they, or their company, may never be known widely, but their service, or product, or legacy may explode after them. This is also scalability—but according to a different definition.

Another example of scalability can be found in the Afrobeat scene, which is now exploding all over the world. Artists from all over sub-Saharan Africa such as Focalistic, Shatta Wale, Davido, Yemi Alade, Wizkid, Aya Nakamura, Salatiel, and Fuse ODG feature on most mainstream radio stations, on celebrity playlists, and in collaborations with artists like Drake, Stormzy, Kanye West, Ed Sheeran, and Beyonce. Burna Boy, the Nigerian superstar, even headlined the concert Citizen of the World in New York late last year, and Afrobeat superstars regularly fill and sell out shows in stadiums and venues as large as the O2 in London, the Madison Square Garden in New York, and even the World Expo in Dubai.

But the seeds of this were irrevocably sown by one man over fifty years ago you've possibly never heard of.

Fela Aníkúlápó Kuti (1938-1997).

The undisputed king of Afrobeat.

Rovi says of Fela on Spotify: "It's almost impossible to overstate the impact and importance of Fela to the global music village: producer, arranger, musician, political radical, outlaw. He was all that, as well as showman par excellence and the inventor of Afrobeat."[5]

Like Welshly Arms, who remains relatively unknown despite the prevalence of their songs in popular culture, the popularity of Afrobeat today started from an artist whose scope was not so large.

Of course, I realize Fela was well known and incredibly popular during his lifetime. The reason I said what I did is that it points to the fact that some readers, especially the younger generation, Africans who have lived most of their lives in the diaspora and new converts to the genre, may not have heard of him even if they've been exposed to Afrobeat through other artists. And every Afrobeat artist, particularly the ones mentioned above, owe their fame to this one man.

How big do you want to go? Is one store enough? Is reaching one country enough? Is one school enough? Does your chosen market (and principles) limit your scalability? Are you prepared to pay the price of virtual anonymity for your service or product to make an impact beyond your dreams? Unfortunately, in an unfair and unbalanced world, these questions do matter.

And as leadership guru Peter Drucker says, the only way for a great future is to create it.[6] But what does 'great' mean? Scalability in business can help us bring greater clarity to this question. In this regard, we might also think about different definitions of success.

Winston Rodney, the Grammy-award-winning reggae artist most popularly known as Burning Spear, is one prime example. Born in Saint Ann's Bay, Jamaica in 1948, Winston has illuminated Rastafarianism in song, sharing his beliefs as part historian, poet, singer, and advocate. He started singing and performing but languished in obscurity until 1976 when he and his

---

5 https://open.spotify.com/artist/5CG9X521RDFWCuAhlo6QoR
6 Williamson, John 1986, The Leader-Manager New York, Page 149, John Wiley and Sons

band released the *Marcus Garvey* album, which took Jamaica by storm and has been hailed as one of the greatest reggae albums ever released.

It was only then that the famous Island label signed Burning Spear on, and Winston had his chance for major mainstream success. However, Island Records infuriated Burning Spear by immediately remixing the album to make it more palatable for white audiences, at the expense of the raw roots sound the album originally had. Winston had pitched his tent. And that came at the expense of mainstream success in 1976. Now, in 2021, Winston is still making music. And no reggae fan will not have heard of Burning Spear. He stuck to his guns. And time rewarded him for it.

Others still are not even well-known till after their death. Take for instance the famous English poet William Blake. It's hard to imagine now that he was virtually unknown during his lifetime because his poems have permeated every sphere of British life and beyond. I sometimes feel that if he were to be here, even he would be shocked at the extent to which his poetry has become a part of the world 400 years later.

QUESTIONS:
1. Where have you had to make decisions about scalability in the creation of your own business model? How did you think about it?

THE PAIN AND PROCESS OF THE FORMATIVE PERIOD

Your joy is your sorrow unmasked....

Some of you say, 'Joy is greater than sorrow,'
and others say, 'Nay, sorrow is the greater.'

But I say unto you, they are inseparable.

Together they come, and when one sits, alone with you at your board,
remember that the other one is asleep upon your bed.

\- Kahlil Gibran, *The Prophet*, 1923

I had that inevitable, fateful call on 3 October, 2019.

As a British-African living in the diaspora with the majority of my family back in my native Ghana, there is something we all share in common.

The fear of the early-morning call.

Earlier that year, I had lost my business, narrowly averted bankruptcy, and, having been duped out of tens of thousands of pounds (now running into millions), was forced to take on a debt repayment plan. I'd lost my first niece, my father-in-law, suffered repeated epileptic attacks, and was too broke to even afford a bus ticket to go to work. My marriage was teetering on the brink due to some bad decisions I'd made. In sum, the chickens had come home to roost.

That call was to say I had suddenly lost my only sister, Glenda, who suffered a suspected stroke. She was perfectly healthy the day before.

The straw that broke the camel's back.

That triggered another attack the next morning as I went on a morning walk alone to clear my thoughts. I picked myself off the pavement and felt blood running down my skull. Another fit.

I had hit my second rock bottom.

Apart from the pain of losing her, how on earth were my brother and I going to raise the thousands of pounds needed to give her the fitting burial she deserved?

That's when the seeds of the poem at the beginning of this book were sown. Glenda's funeral, as painful and heart-breaking as it was, served as the catalyst for the resurrection of BlueCloud Health.

Because, last week, I signed a million-dollar deal with a UK manufacturer and one of West Africa's biggest medicinal distributors for the exclusive rights for manufacturing, distribution, and retailing of medicines and the construction of a manufacturing facility that would supply much of the subcontinent. This happened the very next day.

Failure is never final unless we allow it to be. Our response to the pain we pass through during these formative moments will determine how far we go, what we become, and if we succeed. It's a pain we will have to live with for the rest of our careers, a pain that hopefully will always direct us to true north, a pain that will always remind us of why we do what we do. In short, it is a pain oriented by the love of humanity. I talk about pain and dissect its parts a lot more later on in the book, but it's worth noting that pain in entrepreneurship is guaranteed, a marmite relationship of resilience entrepreneurs will have to cultivate to overcome its inevitability.

If we don't self-sabotage, allow the decisions of others to divert our course, or lose life or limb in the process, it is likely that we will beat the odds and emerge from the ashes—*but only if our foundations are strong enough.*

If there's one principle, just one that you learn from picking up this book, it is this:

<u>We cannot have strong foundations if we haven't gone through the mill. The process. The highs and the lows, the plan and the pain. This dark side of entrepreneurship is not highlighted enough, if at all. And I believe it's the reason why most of us fall by the wayside.</u>

In their book, *Mission: How the Best in Business Break Through*, Michael Hayman and Nick Giles write:

> The prospect of failure always stalks the progress and growth of your business… only by giving your ideas a go can you discover whether they're going to work or not. Treat failure as part of the business cycle; learn from them and keep on moving. It will be the attitude towards the mistakes you make that will define you and your business.[7]

Failure is in some form absolutely guaranteed. As to whether you make it permanent or temporary, that is, in the most part, up to you.

QUESTIONS:

1. Think of a time you failed or had to see your way through significant adversity. What helped you to navigate the most trying moments?

---

7 Hayman & Giles, Mission: How the best in business break through. (London, Random House, UK 2015) pg 200-201

STRUCTURE

If this book works as I've intended, it will be comprehensive enough to serve as a textbook for business students and accessible enough to be read by aspiring entrepreneurs.

It's also meant to be relevant, not just to entrepreneurs of a particular geographic or cultural location, but across cultures. Paradoxically, working in Africa, which harbours some of the world's fastest-growing economies, has been a crucible in which most of the ideas in this book have been formed—and I believe these ideas are extremely relevant lifelong lessons that the world of business can learn from.

More specifically, working in Africa has unparalleled advantages in terms of formulating models. It is not only the fast-growing nature of its economies, but its continually evolving institutions that provide a fascinating backdrop for making business decisions. A lot of models I introduce here have been put to the test and refined through periods of trial and error while operating in that environment—failing forward, as John Maxwell, the bestselling author and leadership guru, puts it.

To further buttress this point, Strive Masiyiwa, whom I quoted earlier and talk about later, makes this point:

> In Africa, a company such as ours often has had to innovate out of necessity. As such we have to do things from scratch. We have managed to leapfrog traditional technologies.
>
> In general, African companies demonstrate far greater adaptability to technological changes than companies in some developed markets. Consequently, you will

see companies that come out of Africa become world champions thanks to this practical approach to innovation.[8]

And Baron Nigel Crisp, former chief executive of the British National Health Service (NHS), in his book *Turning the World Upside Down: The Search for Global Health in the 21ˢᵗ Century*, contends that Africa has a lot of lessons to teach the developed world in healthcare delivery by virtue of the ways it innovates in the midst of severe difficulties.[9]

Another aspect of Africa that is quite interesting given the topic of this book is trust. For instance, in the runaway bestselling book, *Why Nations Fail*, Daron Acemoglu and James Robinson write:

> It might be true that Africans trust each other less than people in other parts of the world. But this is an outcome of a long history of institutions which have undermined human and property rights in Africa. The potential to be captured and sold as a slave no doubt influenced the extent in which Africans trusted themselves historically.[10]

Returning to my earlier description of Africa as a crucible, we can see the way it puts the principles of ethical entrepreneurship to the test, since by definition, integrity, stewardship, legacy, and other crucial tenets of an ethical entrepreneur depend squarely on trust. So, the fact that most of this book is based on events in Africa is, in my estimation, a plus, not a minus.

In addition to looking to the rich context that national, cultural, and institutional realities can provide, I firmly believe that we should reach out to other, sometimes unconventional, models to guide us. In this book, you will encounter repeated forays into arts, sciences, music, stories, and poetry, as well as examples from all over the world. These models will help us to observe underlying principles, much in the way that stories sometimes

---

8 https://www.egonzehnder.com/video/always-be-conscious-that-you-are-setting-a-tone-and-a-value-system-how-strive-masiyiwa-empowers-africa

9 Crisp, Nigel, *Turning the world upside down: the search for global health in the 21st Century*, (London, CRC Press 2010)

10 Acemoglu & James, Why Nations Fail: The Origins of Power, Prosperity and Poverty, (London, Profile Books, 2013)

convey similar messages, even though their appearance, shaped by culture and the author's idiosyncrasies, may appear quite different.

This approach is not new.

In one of the best books I've ever read, *Farsighted: How We Make the Decisions That Matter the Most*, bestselling author Steven Johnson writes:

> When you read literature as an exercise in improving our ability to make farsighted decisions, you can appreciate the way novels mirror the scientific insights that arise from randomised controlled studies and ensemble forecasts, in their shared reliance on the power of simulation to expand our perspectives, challenge our assumptions, and propose new possibilities.
>
> This is not a matter of "reducing" the humanities down to scientific data. **For the most intimate decisions, novels (and I would include poetry, music, movies, and stories—emphasis mine)** endow us with wisdom that science cannot, by definition provide. You don't get to run ensemble simulations on your own life. Storytelling is what we have as a substitute.
>
> Of course, the reverse is also true: science gives us insights that novels cannot provide… novels just happen to shine a different kind of light**….we see further when both lights are on** (emphasis mine).[11]

I stumbled across this book on a family holiday in Hay-On-Wye, Wales, known for its famous annual literary festival. It lay dormant until I happened to pick it up in the midst of writing this book, and it explained in detail what I was already doing.

Steven Johnson used George Eliot's classic novel, *Middlemarch*, first published in 1871, as a guide for a major personal decision he had to make and dedicates a whole chapter to explaining how he did so.

---

11 Johnson, Steven, Farsighted: How we make the decisions that matter the most, (New York, Riverhead Books, 2018)

To take just one example from this book, I use insights from the periodic table of the elements to explain how we should choose our business partners, including criteria to use and ways to enforce contracts, as well as Rutherford's gold foil experiment to discount the theory of the plum pudding model of the atom to explain the process of validating your business idea. But I also use lots of stories based on, and inspired by, real events to buttress and, where necessary, clarify these points. Both used together, I find, work better synergistically than 'scientific research' used that may or may not be filled with halos.

Steven Johnson's model, I thus find, might be a much better way to describe business principles I use in this book, rather than using loads of loads of 'research data' using the scientific model used by other bestselling authors such as Jim Collins (*Good to Great, Built to Last*) and Waterman and Peters (of *In Search of Excellence* fame) and more recently *CEO Excellence* by Dewar, Kelhar and Malhotra of McKinsey fame.

This is what Phil Rosenweig calls the '*Delusion of Organizational Physics*'— that the business world conforms to precise and predictable laws. As he says, it fuels a belief that a given set of actions can work in all settings and ignores the need to adapt to different conditions such as intensity of competition, rate of growth, global dispersion of activities, etc. Claiming that one approach can work everywhere, at all times, for all companies has a simplistic appeal, but doesn't do justice to the complexities of business.[12]

I find this all too real in my own experience, where working in the field of toil, sweat, blood, and tears (literally) in Africa has not yielded the same results as it would elsewhere. And this is a common complaint of African, Asian, and Middle Eastern entrepreneurs that I have worked with, which my own experience validates.

And I have given lots of examples in this book to show that.

---

12 Rosenzweig, Phil. The Halo Effect and the Eight Other Business Delusions that Deceive Managers (New York, Free Press, 2007)

Of course, that is not to say these books have no value. Absolutely not. I quote them in this book. I have read each and every one of them and have been incredibly inspired and have gained valuable insights. But I am also aware that they contain halos and are better read as stories, which we need to use in context, rather than as scientific facts, and we all need to recognise this.

Finally, why me?

I was born in London, England, but lived the majority of my life in Ghana, West Africa, studied at one of the best business schools in the world, trained as a community pharmacist, and founded a business that has been responsible for millions of dollars worth of deals in four continents. I believe that my background gives me a context from which to address a broad spectrum of readers without falling into the trap of acting as a jack-of-all-trades.

With that in mind, the structure of the book is divided into three parts. Taken together, they point to different phases of the entrepreneurial journey and provide suggestions for how to navigate them.

- **PART 1: The Honeymoon Period**
  - The Person
  - The Purpose
  - The Passion
- **PART 2: The Formative Period**
  - The Partner
  - The Pain
  - The Payoff
- **PART 3: The Legacy Period**
  - The Power Legacy
  - The Place Legacy
  - The Passover Legacies

So undergirded with these foundations, we are now ready to begin... with the dream, the ignition…. The Honeymoon.

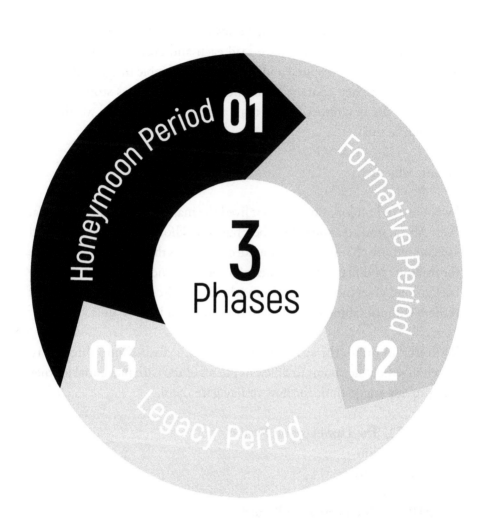

THE HONEYMOON PERIOD

❝...You have to remember, cherish and appreciate the good times to survive through the bad...**❞**

June Lawrence

Yeah
Everybody falls sometimes
Just remember that that's all right
It's the rainy days that give us love for the sun
And if it isn't, I guess I'll be fine believing it does, oh yeah
Everybody falls sometimes
Just remember that that's all right
It's the lows in life that make you cherish the highs
And if isn't, I guess I'll be fine believing a lie, ayy

- NF, "Just Like You," *The Mixtape*, 2020

THE PERSON
WHO IS AN ETHICAL ENTREPRENEUR?

Let's start a fire
Let's pull this trigger
'Cause all these bruises make our skin thicker
Now everybody can see our scars
It's what we're made of
It's who we are
It's what we're made of
It's who we are.....

- Welshly Arms, "Who We Are," *Legendary,* 2019

Holly Bradshaw had finally done it.

After nine major global championships, the 29-year-old British Olympian had finally done it, winning an Olympic bronze medal, Britain's first, in the pole-vault in Tokyo 2020.

For a decade, she had endured the tag of the 'nearly woman' of British athletics, finishing fourth, fifth, sixth in previous competitions, overcoming COVID, losing her Nike sponsorship, and battling injury and depression to finally make the cut. Her live sessions of filming stretching sessions for the followers had even been hijacked by hackers who replaced her class with pornographic imagery.

So, what finally changed? What did she credit her success to?

In an interview documented in *The Telegraph* newspaper in August 2021, she reiterated,

I was picking up on traits I didn't like… Someone would jump really well in America, and I'd be gutted. It would hurt me, and I'd feel sick to my stomach. I didn't like that in myself, so I wanted to change that. I researched it, spoke to my psychologist, and wanted to change myself.

I had to change a lot of my inner values, work on myself, and change stuff to enjoy it more. Since then, I just feel like I love what I'm doing. Whether I come sixth, fourth, first in any competition, it doesn't matter. It's about me jumping, building, enjoying, and building in the last four years.[13]

Inner values. Core strength. Two sides of the same coin.

The perseverance of Holly Bradshaw, exemplified by running in her garden during the first lockdown (months after Nike had cut her sponsorship, by the way) with a baked bean can strapped to a washing pole, is what this book is all about.

You cannot build outer success without building inner success. This is what Gordon MacDonald, in his bestseller, *Ordering Your Private World,* calls "The Private Garden,"[14] which I have adapted to draw out the principles of the ethical entrepreneur.

In 2003, when I had my first managerial job in a small pharmacy in Plymouth, England, a memo from the head office was circulated about what a well-stocked community pharmacy should look like. It had charts, pictures, and diagrams, but the title stuck in my head. It was the first time I had seen it.

The title was WGLL.

WGLL stood for 'what good looks like.'

---

13 https://www.telegraph.co.uk/olympics/2021/08/05/tokyo-olympics-2020-live-athletics-diving-400m-final-gb-bosworth/
14 MacDonald, Gordon. Ordering Your Private World – Key Steps to greater resourcefulness, effectiveness and balance (Nashville 1984 Moody)

The precept was simple. You conducted the revamp of your shop from top to bottom until it approximated the diagrams, charts, and pictures in the memo. The closer the resemblance, the better your retail pharmacy was. In the same vein, it is imperative that we nail down what an ethical entrepreneur is.

I have always been dead against the stereotyped "rags-to-riches" concept of an entrepreneur. Indeed, the term has been romanticised for generations. The lone ranger or young team that defeats all the odds, disrupts the markets, and builds a business that makes millions of dollars It's been popularised through TV programs such as *Dragon's Den* and *The Apprentice* in the UK and *Shark Tank* in the US.

From my point of view, one of the best definitions of an entrepreneur from the hundreds of books, articles, blogs, and reports on the subject I have read (and experienced) comes from Eric Ries in his runaway best-seller *The Lean Startup*: "A startup is a human institution designed to create a new product or service under conditions of extreme uncertainty."

He goes on to say: "Anyone who is creating a new product or business under such conditions is an entrepreneur whether she knows it or not, and whether working in a government agency, a venture-backed company, a nonprofit, or a decidedly for-profit company with financial investors."[15]

And with reference to this concept, I believe that the ethical entrepreneur is defined by five principles:

1. The ethical entrepreneur understands the principle of stewardship

The principle of stewardship means that you have something under your care for a fixed period of time. Even though you invented that product or service, cared for it, nurtured it, and brought it to fruition, you only have a fixed period of time during which you are in charge of it, and eventually,

---

15 Ries, Eric. The Lean Startup (New York, Penguin, 2011)

like a baton in a relay race, you will have to relinquish control. So a big part of your calling, if I can describe it that way, is managing that process and bearing in mind that you have control over how you pass the baton. If you bring this principle to bear on your day-to-day routines, you will be taking a significant step toward what Dr. Henry Cloud calls the transcendent leader in his book, *Integrity: The Courage to Meet the Demands of Reality*:

> The transcendent leader realises that there are things much bigger than her, and her existence is really not just about her and her interests, but ultimately, about the things larger than she is. Her life is about fitting into those things, joining them, serving them, obeying them and finding her role in the big picture. Then as a result, she ultimately becomes a part of them and finds meaning much larger than a life that is just about her. Life is about things that transcend her.[16]

This dovetails nicely into the second principle of the ethical entrepreneur:

2. The ethical entrepreneur understands the principle of identity

Yeah,
Don't take opinions from people that won't listen to yours
If money's where you find happiness, you'll always be poor
If you don't like the job you have, then what do you do it for?
The cure to pain isn't something you buy at liquor stores
The real you is not defined by the size of your office
The real you is who you are when ain't nobody watching
You spend your whole life worried about what's in your wallet
For what? Than money won't show up in your coffin, woo!

- NF, "Remember This," *Perception*

The principle of identity means that there is a separation between who you are and what you do.

---

16 Cloud, Henry. Integrity: The Courage to Meet the Demands of Reality (New York, HarperCollins 2006)

This is diametrically opposed to being preoccupied with accomplishment and its corresponding symbols: status, titles, office location, material objects.

This is what Holly Bradshaw learnt in the four years after Rio (which paradoxically gave her the success she craved) and what many leaders, dictators and people of great influence have failed to learn.

And losing sight of this separation is why people who have enjoyed great power and privilege find it almost impossible to give it up after their time of stewardship has passed and will fight to the death to retain what they had.

From the standpoint of the principle of identity, it's easy to see why leaders like Nelson Mandela, Mahatma Gandhi, and Sir Alex Ferguson are almost universally acclaimed. They gave it up voluntarily when they figured it was time to go, when their period of stewardship was coming to a close. They refused to allow a messianic fantasy to infect their leadership style and remembered that they have the same biological composition as the average Joe down the road. Journaling and personal meditation are crucial for cultivating this standpoint.

It is the very same thing that gave them the strength to resist destructive behaviours towards other people when things didn't go their way or they sensed disloyalty, criticism, or opposition. Instead, they could concentrate rather on building, not tearing down. They spent time reflecting on, reinforcing, and refining their internal values, their true north, their identity.

But that's not all.

Your identity also reflects your core beliefs—who you really are as a person. This will feed into every decision you make as an entrepreneur.

Climate change? Women's rights? Racial and sexual discrimination? Eradication of poverty? You can use these things as a gimmick for so long, but if making people and the planet better isn't a core of what you really believe in, it will show up, and show your company up. It all starts with your core identity—what you really believe deep down.

And what you believe should lead to a deep, deep reservoir of self-belief, that you belong, and that you deserve a seat at the table. Not because you're better than anybody else, or that you're the best thing since sliced bread, but that what you have to offer fits into a grand **purpose** that will benefit humanity in some positive way.

3. The ethical entrepreneur understands the principle of purpose

I always smile when I see on TV in the UK the advert showing The Barclaycard Sidekicks.

The sidekick understands his role: "As a sidekick to a hero, my role is to help whenever I can."

I was privileged to serve as a best man for one of my closest and long-time friends, Brian Martin.

My purpose, then, was to make sure that all the attention belonged to him and to his new spouse, Anna, not to me. I had to remind myself of this throughout the wedding ceremony.

We look more at purpose later on in this book, but the idea is that what we commit ourselves to should be something that benefits humanity, and that fills us with a sense of destiny, without allowing ourselves, our pride, or our egos to get in the way.

I was reminded of this when our firm, Emerald, was working towards financing a multimillion deal in Ghana. This deal had the potential to preserve thousands of jobs and continue to maintain Ghana as one of the premier producers of cocoa in the world. The deal involved working with professionals from four continents who came together for the purpose of closing this deal.

There were continuous clashes: egos, pride, insults, time zones, different cultural experiences, and language barriers. The deal was in constant danger of being derailed. All parties said and did things which were regrettable, myself included. The biggest difficulty was not closing the deal but getting people to look beyond their narrow self-interests and focus on the result.

Extremely tough, especially in this world of me, me, me.

Eventually, the egos of all parties got in the way, and a potential deal worth hundreds of millions of dollars was lost at the last hurdle despite our best efforts.

Because they keep their eyes on the purpose, ethical entrepreneurs tend to be highly collaborative, specialise in harnessing people's strengths, and concentrate on win-win situations to achieve end results that are beneficial for everybody.

4. The ethical entrepreneur understands the principle of the trail

I am my own father
But that wasn't always clear
I had to learn my duties, fast
It wasn't easy.
I got some lines on my face
I got a battle with the booze
I look prettier that I am,
But there's a talent to that.

- Yrsa Daley-Ward, "Skill," *Bone*, 2017

What is the principle of the trail?

Wherever we go, work or live, we leave a trail behind us. And that trail is made up of two things, our compassion and our competence. And these are the two things that we will always be judged by.

Our compassion reflects how we treat people we work with, including our board, employees, shareholders, partners, and customers.

This extends to a crucial trait of the ethical entrepreneur: they love people, are sensitive to their needs, and are committed to creating environments where people who work and live with them can thrive and fulfil their own dreams.

Sadly, this is becoming more infrequent. You only need to look at many powerful leaders in our world and the destructive trail of bodies they leave in their wake as they climb the ladder of success.

One of my favourite quotes about it is from Guy Raz's *How I Built This*:

> Fundamentally, I don't believe a company can stand the test of time if people will not stand for the company. And I find one of the most reliable ways the vast majority of entrepreneurs inspire people is to do with kindness…. they treat their people well. They do the little things and the big things. They pay their success forward.

He continues:

> And with rare exceptions, they are also highly ethical. They act with an integrity that seems to come from a place of deep morality…. they are compassionate. There is an empathy present in their decisions that often extends all the way out to the customer.[17]

If there is one trail I'd like to leave and be remembered by, it would be that I was kind.

However, loving people must also be balanced by loving the job we do and being damn good at it. At the end of the day, we are hired to do a job, whether as an entrepreneur, an employee, a board member, or a partner. And that job has to be done to the highest standard possible.

---

17 Raz, Guy, How I Built This: The Unexpected Paths to Success from the World's Most Inspiring Entrepreneurs (London, MacMillan, 2020)

You have to be good at what you do.

And you must set a dynamic standard to continually improve, learn, get better. And expect high standards from your partners, employees, colleagues, everyone you work with. We talk more about this later in the book with the concept of personal capacity.

This is encapsulated in one word: competence.

THE TRAIL = COMPASSION + COMPETENCE

It's funny, but one of my proudest moments is also possibly one of my most mundane and least headline-grabbing.

I was hired as a consultant community pharmacist during the first lockdown in the UK in a community pharmacy that had just got through an inspection and nearly failed.

A small team of six staff worked to deliver 500 COVID tests, 7,500 monthly prescriptions, and numerous other services including emergency contraception, mobility services, and over-the-counter services, as well as thousands of vaccines for the flu and COVID every month.

But what's different about this team?

Its diversity.
- A devout, fashion-crazy, fragile young Muslim who came to the UK as a refugee from Kurdistan.
- A vivacious, impulsive, white, openly gay young millennial with a passion for people, cars, and her pimped-up Audi A3.
- A Christian, disorganised, black British of African origin who loves hip-hop and grime.
- A compassionate and sensitive single mother who loves to ride horses and build people up.

- A bisexual Yorkshire 25-year-old woman with a master's degree in oceanography.
- Two British Asians of Indian origin.
- A middle-aged, single, quintessential British white woman.

As diverse as diverse could be. But united in one quest.

To transform a 40-year-old pharmacy that nearly got shut down into one that delivered great pharmaceutical service in a city that was almost 99 percent white in a year where doom and gloom filled the country and businesses all around us were closing daily.

And I was privileged to lead this team. To start from the bottom up and to invest my time personally into each and every one of them. Pay them well. Secure their future. Goad, persuade, and coach them to unify around the steely determination to keep things moving during unbelievably hard times.

Practically speaking, this looked like supporting a member when they had to fast during Ramadan, helping another keep her equestrian passion going during the week, and being with another who had just endured a painful breakup with her partner.

18 months later and the turnaround is complete. 60 percent increase in revenue, a glowing inspection from the UK pharmacy regulator, a happy team, and, most of all, praise and a retail pharmacy packed to the rafters with returning customers.

So, people matter, but the job also matters. Be kind, but also be skilful.

The overriding caveat: gentleness.

The Greek word for gentleness is ευγένεια.

And it encapsulates the overriding principle here.

In the trail, both for compassion and competence, gentleness is key.

In the Greek, it conveys an attitude of all-encompassing kindness when retaliation is to be expected, rather than vengeful retribution. People that are vengeful to other people are not normally gentle with themselves either.

But in the same vein, do not be afraid to get people off the bus who consistently and persistently mess up with compassion. Or competence, for that matter.

We will cover this in greater detail later in the book, under The Payoff.

5. The Ethical Entrepreneur Understands the Principle of Stickability

The whale is your unwritten book,
your unsung song, your calling....
You die grappling with this thing, lashed to it,
battling it even as it takes you under...[18]

  - Steven Pressfield, *The White Whale*

This last principle depends on and is mastered through the other four. Though they act as the foundation for stickability, stewardship, identity, purpose, and the trail are not enough. If you believe in in these principles, you must be prepared to live (and die) by them.

It is not enough to know who you are. Understand that you are just a steward and be convinced of your purpose, your mission.

But it's crucial to stick with it if you believe in it.

Stickability is a marriage of commitment and perseverance.

---

18 Pressfield, Steven, The War of Art (New York, Black Irish Books 2002)

STICKABILITY = COMMITMENT + PERSEVERANCE

In my own life, I have had to live this out. It is a decision, a commitment, something that you 'pitch your tent' on.

Plain grit. Doing the work.

That's why the Honeymoon Period looms so large in the structure of this book. And it is something I'm absolutely convinced about.

It's why I have stuck with BlueCloud despite two car accidents in which the vehicles were destroyed beyond reasonable repair, near bankruptcy, sleeping rough, incredible betrayal, loneliness, severe health problems, legal threats and severe financial, relational and resource challenges, and a whole decade with no meaningful paycheck.

And its why I am always inspired by stories such as Holly Bradshaw's and countless others who have blazed the trail before us. And like Holly, these can only be forged by you.

So this is WGLL. Our true north, our compass, our ideas. And the foundation, the raison d'être for this book.

But all this comes to nothing if you don't know the why. Why are you doing this? What is all this hassle for? Money is important, but is it all that there is? There needs to be, as I have introduced in the five principles, a purpose.

And it's to this that we turn next.

KEY CONCEPTS:
1. WGLL

2. Stewardship, Identity, Purpose, The Trail, and Stickability

QUESTIONS:

1. Do you have a model for WGLL? If so, what is it? If not, how would you start thinking about it?

2. Which of the five principles do you identify with most?

3. Which of the five principles could become a potential area of growth?

THE PURPOSE

Here we are with our desperate youth and the pain
We're awakening
Maybe it's called ambition when you've been talking in your sleep
About a dream
We're awakening...

- Switchfoot, "Awakening," *Oh! Gravity*, 2005

**"In the journey to success,
the tenacity of purpose is supreme."**
- Aliko Dangote, billionaire entrepreneur and founder
of the Dangote Group of companies

Ping!

The idea.

This is the birth-point. When it all starts. When the key is put into the ignition and the car starts. This is when you have the idea, spot the market need, see the gap that needs to be filled, when you have the aha! moment.

Or, like me, a vague sense of destiny, a calling to make your little corner of the world a better place by building a successful business and going on a quest to find it.

The importance of this has been stressed, and rightly so, throughout the literature. And for many of us, it comes in different ways—a dream, a tragedy, an unfulfilled need, from a book or from countless other sources.

As I write this, my daughter, Nshira, has just won the most outstanding enterprising student in her key stage group in the whole of the UK for 2021.

Her idea is incredibly simple, which most brilliant inventions seem to be—a subscription model app which showcases the rich diversity of the world to a paying customer—in an age where so much information is freely available, but so little learning is done; an age where we seem to have lost all sense of sharing, of listening, of understanding, of reaching out across the aisle.

As a father, I am incredibly proud, of course.

But it also highlights a very obvious fact.

The idea is not the issue.

How likely is it that my daughter can turn this idea she birthed with her team into a million-dollar thriving business that solves one of the world's pressing problems— racism, bigotry, and distrust?

What are the odds that two years from now that idea will be buried in the bowels of her Lenovo laptop under a pile of documents, subjects, downloads, and papers in preparation for her A-levels? That the award she received would just be gathering dust on her shelf beside one of her most prized possessions, a vinyl by Tyler the Creator? The idea is not the issue.

Chances are that if you've picked up this book, or you have had to buy it for a course, you have a good idea of the business you want to start.

But even if you don't, it's okay because it will find you. How do you know it's the one? Your heart beats faster every time it comes to you. It scares you to death, but you are strangely convinced and compelled. It keeps you up in the dead of night. It tells you that there is something more, that you weren't made for the mundane, simple life you're now living.

For Tony Kofi, the famous award-winning Ghanaian-British saxophonist, the prospect of death literally turned his life around.

It was spring 1981, and the 16-year-old carpentry apprentice in Nottingham, England was working on replacing the old roof of a house. He wanted to impress so badly that he offered to work during his lunch break.

He was three stories high and was sawing a two-by-four length of wood. "I didn't saw it properly, and it splintered," he recalls, speaking on a recent podcast on BBC Sounds with Jane Garvey.[19]

"It caught my sleeve and took me down," he added.

He began to fall. He thought to himself, "I'm going to die. There's no way I can survive this." So, he completely relaxed, let go, and closed his eyes.

That's the moment his purpose found him.

As he was falling, pictures and visions flashed through his eyes. People he'd never seen. Images of places to which he'd never travelled. But the big one—he was standing up and playing an instrument. An instrument he'd never seen in his life.

Then everything went black.

After three weeks in hospital with a cracked skull, severe head trauma, and severe emotional stress, he was sent home to recover with compensation and an open invitation to go back to work.

But he couldn't shake the image of the instrument from his mind. He was obsessed, and he'd kept it to himself for obvious reasons. He had no idea what the instrument was.

---

19 'The near death experience that made me a musician – BBC Radio 4 Life Changing https://www.bbc.co.uk/programmes/m000w33t

He finally went through numerous pictures in books about instruments and found out what he'd been seeing.

A saxophone.

So, he used all his compensation, £50 (around £500 pounds in today's money), bought one, quit his carpentry job, and started practicing, sometimes for 8 to 10 hours a day. He refused to go back to his job despite pleas from his parents.

His parents thought the fall had messed up his head.

But he said to his parents, "If you make me go back to carpentry, I might as well have died in that fall." They let him alone after that.

And to make things worse, he got rejected by music schools in the UK because he had no qualifications.

So, one day, about seven years after the incident, he turned his attention to the US and applied to go study at the Berklee College of Music in Boston, Massachusetts, one of the most prestigious music schools in the world.

And they let him in, with an audition, but without any qualifications. So, in 1988, the then-24-year-old left the UK to study music.

After his graduation, his first album, *All Is Know*, won the BBC Jazz Award in 2005. Then the awards kept coming. Another award in 2008. An honorary professorship from Nottingham University. A 2008 MOBO nomination and a Presto Music award in 2020.

Not bad for a 16-year-old, music-illiterate carpenter apprentice.

I shudder to think what would have happened if he had just done nothing about that experience and gone back to being a carpenter as, no doubt, 99 percent of people would probably have done.

You may be slaving now in a sell-out job, or a shadow career, as Steven Pressfield calls it. You may be jumping from place to place or career to career.

But there will be always be a conviction that scares you to death, won't let you go, that grapples with you all day and night.

The issue is what will you do with the idea or conviction? Will it be relegated to the back shelves of your mind as a relic of the past? Will you even remember that you had an idea five years from now?

There is a war raging, and you have to make a choice.

What you do with that idea will determine the path you take.

You need to take that first step.

I had my ping! moment 15 years ago, working as a community pharmacist in Plymouth, Devon, Southwest England.

It wasn't a concrete idea. It was just a nagging conviction, that I had to do more than travel round working in pharmacies across the country.

It had already been a gruelling journey to get to this point. A journey that started in 1992, in Accra, Ghana.

I had failed my A-levels. Twice.

The original idea my father had was to get me into medicine, to become a doctor. I came from a typical African middle-class family where the prescription was clear. GCSEs, A-levels, university, then becoming a lawyer, doctor, or engineer.

My grades were not good enough to get me into university, let alone study medicine. After the second attempt, I scraped through with a D in Physics. Just enough to get me into pharmacy.

After my degree, I decided to come to the United Kingdom to practice after working as a pharmacist in Ghana for just over a year. I wasn't getting the fulfilment I felt in Ghana, and I thought life in the UK would be better and afford me more opportunities. What's more, I was a British citizen but had never really visited apart from a stint in 1985 for a four-week holiday. So I left, and two years later, in 2000, I was the proud recipient of a certificate that allowed me to practice pharmacy in the United Kingdom, a profession I would stick with for 20 years.

I married my long-time girlfriend from Ghana, bought a nice home in the peaceful, sleepy city of Plymouth, and started my family. Life was good.

But after the fourth year of practicing, the old discontent I felt in Ghana began to resurface. The vague conviction that I had to do more. To start my own business. And no, it wasn't a pharmacy—to buy a pharmacy chain as some of my colleagues had done.

I didn't know what it was, but the tug wouldn't go away.

Finally, in 2008, I gave in and applied to do an MBA at one of the UK's top business schools, Warwick Business School. My family thought I was mad.

It was an amazing experience, one of the best. I met some of the most brilliant minds, learnt a ton of stuff, and made lifelong friends.

I was wide-eyed and drooling at the prospect of life after business school.

After 2010, Africa began to finally boom, and investment was pouring into the continent. Democracy was beginning to take hold. There was real hope, real belief that finally, after many false starts, the continent was ready to take off. Rwanda had turned the corner. Ghana had found oil and, like Zambia, was now a middle-income country. South Africa had successfully hosted the FIFA World Cup. Nigeria's economy was overtaking South Africa as Africa's biggest. Mobile money, led by Kenya's M-Pesa, and a telecommunication boom were surging across the continent. Many books were being written on the new Africa. Record Africans from the diaspora were returning to start their own businesses or work.

This new optimism about Africa was summarised by the flying headline in *The Economist* December 3rd, 2011 edition entitled, "The Hopeful Continent."

After decades of slow growth, Africa had a real chance to follow in the footsteps of Asia.

I remember the words from Dr. Ngozi Okonjo-Iweala. Then Minister of Finance of Nigeria, and now the current head of the World Trade Organisation, she said in her foreword to *The Fastest Billion* by Charles Robertson of Renaissance Capital:

> After decades of genuine struggle, Africa's time has arrived, and its people are crying out to be recognised. Africa, as this book's title rightly projects, will be quickest to succeed. The question for global investors and international policy makers is whether they want to share in the profits. Africa will indeed claim its due, and global capital markets will play a vital role. [20]

Those words, penned a decade ago now, spurred me on then, and still spur me on now—and confirmed what I had been believing for some time: a burgeoning middle class was emerging in Africa.

With the skills I had learned from business school, the contacts I had met, my background as a healthcare professional, and my ethnicity as a Black British man with Ghanaian heritage, I felt I was ready to make the jump.

So, in the final year, I had the ping! moment. Business school had distilled all my vague surmising into a crystal-clear idea, and BlueCloud Healthcare was born.

---

20 Robertson, Moran, Mhango et al, The Fastest Billion: The Story Behind Africa's Economic Revolution (London, Renaissance Capital, 2012)

I had the idea—the mission:

"BlueCloud Health will exist to provide new ethical, sustainable, and profitable healthcare investment opportunities for small and middle healthcare businesses in Sub-Saharan Africa and, in so doing, increase the life expectancy and substantially improve healthcare outcomes for all Africans."

I didn't know it then, but I had started the journey, the model in this book. And one more thing I didn't know then. It would take a full decade to get BlueCloud's first proper deal in the bag and the corresponding money in the account.

But how did I know that this idea would work?

Validation.

THE POWER OF VALIDATION—THE CAMEL PRINCIPLE

The 'I told you so' moment.

I remember that night on June 28, 2019 like it was yesterday.

We sat open-mouthed as Stormzy, the iconic British Grime and hip-hop rapper, took to the Pyramid stage to headline the famous Glastonbury festival. I remember beaming from ear to ear as he climbed onto the stage with his Union Jack stab vest.

Grime had arrived on the mainstream.

The doubter list was long and loud.

With just one album under his belt, people questioned whether he was ripe for the big stage.

But he proved them wrong, and then some.

In his incredible, breath-taking performance, hailed the world over, he rattled off a long list of grime artists, past and present, 52 in total, who had silently been slaving away for decades.

Because they had validated the genre before him, made all the mistakes, carried all the burdens, he knew he had what it took.

In an interview in *TIME* magazine, where he made its cover as a next-generation leader, he said:

> I know I'm the product of bare injustice. There are so many iconic, legendary, more influential grime songs that are never going to sell as much records as I've sold. This is why I'm always so thankful for being in the position I am. I feel like all those artists or public figures or celebrities who went through that, had to go through that… they didn't have the luxury of being free with their music, **and they had to bite that bullet for me** (emphasis mine). So, I love and respect all those people, for all their decisions.[21]

All those 52 artists before him had validated the genre of grime. And Stormzy was riding the wave. And he was humble enough to recognise that.

In The Lean Startup, Eric Ries talks about taking a prototype of your raw-form product to test. This book extends his principle of validation. The idea is that in these starry-eyed times, you are aware that hard times will come, so you are building up as much fat as possible now.

I have called this the Camel Principle:

The ethical entrepreneur will only have enough strength to last in the Formative Period as he has stored up in the Honeymoon.

---

21 https://time.com/collection/next-generation-leaders/5692968/stormzy-next-generation-leaders/

The idea here is you are making sure you are convinced in your inner being that this course you have taken is worth the wait, worth the pain, worth the sacrifice.

There are six primary ways your idea and future business can be validated:
1. Through journaling and reflection
2. Through affirmation
3. Through research
4. Through testing and trial
5. Beginning with the end in mind
6. Passing the four ethical pillars test

VALIDATION BY JOURNALING AND REFLECTION

Fast checks, fast women that don't inspire me, no!
You don't wanna know what's going on inside my personal life?
Then get out my diary, yeah,
I wanna know what it's like to be happy.....

- NF, "Know," *Perception*, 2020

Keeping a journal is crucial and a must, especially in the early stages of your dream. It is important that all your ideas are recorded, and regular time is set aside for it. Your journal must include everything you have in mind: your dreams, your feelings, your excitement about the idea, and everything in between.

Ideas have a way of disentangling themselves when they are put in ink. You will never be able to validate your purpose unless it is written out. Once it is on paper, it is separated from you and then takes on a life of its own.

Waking up early in the morning, before everyone else, and devoting time to reading, meditation, and writing is crucial.

There has been a solid body of research that has attested to the benefits of journaling, and I think the best way is simply to do it.

I love writing with pen and paper, but there are hundreds of apps that can help facilitate the process.

I have kept detailed journals for over 20 years of my life.

Much of this book was written by hand in several journals. So was the poetry and even the music. It's amazing what can come out of you when you make time for this indispensable habit.

My friend, Claire Oatway, executive coach and CEO of leadership consultancy Neon Juno, said in her interview in the August 2021 issue of *Authority Magazine*:

> Journal it. If you've got a busy head, then write it out. If it's a to-do list—get it written down. You don't need to remember everything, and it all takes up mental energy. If you have a gut feeling or worry, write it out—seeing the words in front of you can help you evaluate whether they are accurate and help you problem-solve more objectively. Actively writing allows a subconscious flow and can stop a thought from bouncing like a pinball in your head.[22]

This is confirmed by an article in the *Harvard Business Review*, which emphasises how using a pen to write in a journal "seems to be the speed with which my imagination finds the best," according to novelist Paul Theroux. Dan Ciampa, the author of the article, says that "the best thinking comes from structured reflection—and the best way to do that is keeping a personal journal."[23]

VALIDATION BY RESEARCH

Selling Interactions is a UK-based sales consulting firm with a presence in over 14 countries who counts scores of world-class companies among their clients, including Volvo, Cushman and Wakefield, and Interroll. Selling

---

22 https://medium.com/authority-magazine/beating-burnout-claire-oatway-on-the-5-things-you-should-do-if-you-are-experiencing-work-burnout-2c29633f6158
23 https://hbr.org/2017/07/the-more-senior-your-job-title-the-more-you-need-to-keep-a-journal?utm_medium=social&utm_campaign=hbr&utm_source=LinkedIn&tpcc=orgsocial_edit

Interactions was set up in 2010 with a very simple philosophy—search relentlessly for sales best practices and use the insights to help clients improve their sales organisations and ultimately their sales.

Anderson Hirst, the CEO and founder of the company, developed a passion for evidence-based selling when working as a consultant advising Skoda on their sales approach. He noticed there was no defined sales practice with proven results, and he had an idea on how to develop one.

The result was the Sales Excellence Diagnostic blueprint, a product of three years of research culminating in a distinction from the Warwick Business School. The Sales Excellence Diagnostic was his dissertation for his MBA.

The results speak for themselves —companies that have worked with Selling Interactions have boasted up to 70 percent increase in sales turnover.

The youthful gleam and passion in his eyes when we met for coffee was inspiring, infectious, and... I must confess, annoying. How could anyone have so much passion for... selling? But I couldn't shake off the stardust in his eyes. And I'm glad I didn't. Because that cup of coffee on that cold winter morning in Coventry in 2013 with Anderson cemented and formed the blueprint for my own project in the same business school, with the same results.

It formed the bedrock for BlueCloud and partially sowed the seeds for the book you now hold in your hands.

Anderson has done this for me and hundreds of other MBA students. His passion, apart from helping companies sell better, is delivering talks, seminars, and conferences, both in-person and virtually, to entrepreneurs on the importance of validation by research. He has developed the concept of the sweet spot—the diagram of which is shown on the following page.

YOUR STRENGTHS
What of your skills add most
value to organisations?
What are you good at
already?

CAREER VALUE
What expertise will you
need in your next role?
What will the market value?

SWEET
SPOT

YOUR LIKES
What type of work do you
like? What topics & ways
of working do you enjoy?

VALIDATION BY PIVOTING

I remember that day in Lagos, Nigeria in October 2014.

After around an hour in crippling traffic, driving through the sweltering heat of Sub-Saharan Africa's biggest city, we finally arrived at a tiny office to meet two young entrepreneurs, Chibuzo Opara and Adham Yehia, founders of DrugStoc, a new startup dedicated to ending the epidemic of fake medicines streaming into the country. A recent study from the PWC and an article from the Financial Times had shown that up to 70 percent of the medicines entering the developing countries were either fake or substandard, and Nigeria was the world's biggest counterfeit market.

As my business partner Abhinav and I stood in their tiny office and listened to their vision, we could not help but wonder how these two bright-faced young ethical entrepreneurs were going to take on this seemingly insurmountable challenge that partly emanated from the corruption and ambivalence of upper echelons of the ruling elite of Africa's biggest economy.

Our investment partners were even more sceptical. Despite our best efforts, we were unable to raise the money they needed.

Fast forward to August 2021.

DrugStoc have now moved into a 3,000-square-foot, massive office and are now dispensing over six million prescriptions, and thousands of hospitals and pharmacies now depend on them to supply end-to-end medication, which is quality guaranteed.

They have successfully raised millions of dollars on the open market, are on track to make over $5 million this year, and are winning numerous awards for their unwavering commitment to quality and service.

Their road to success reminded me of Eric Ries *The Lean Startup* again. I caught up with them on a recent conference call, and Adham told me the following:

> In a way, when you came to see us in 2014, DrugStoc was ahead of its time as Nigerians were not used to using apps and ordering medicines online. So, we ran out of money very quickly. But because we were ahead of the market by a few years, we fortunately had the opportunity to make all our mistakes, refine the model and software, tweak the vision, and learn the fundraising cycle. There were also a few customers of ours who were also ahead of the market. They were our 'guinea pigs'—our pilot customers. We are ethical to a fault, so even though there were ways to jump the gun, we stuck to our principles. So, by the time the market was ready, we were ready. We were fortunate not to have gotten that funding then, because even though it was disappointing, in hindsight, we were not prepared.

Now that they have established their model, built trust, and secured the much-needed funding, DrugStoc have detailed plans to rapidly expand to 16 other Nigerian cities by 2024, and plan to expand across other African cities where fake drugs are still a huge problem.

As the example of DrugStoc indicates, pivoting can look like keeping the vision but changing the pace and speed of direction; building capacity and trialling their model on early uptake customers, whilst waiting for the market to catch up. I talk more about this kind of pivoting later on in the book when we delve deeper into the causes of pain in the entrepreneurial journey.

Then there is Goodbody Clinic, here in the UK.

Goodbody Health (formerly Sativa Wellness Group), a UK-based health product company founded in 2019 by entrepreneur Geremy Thomas, was initially known for its brilliant customer service and high-end CBD products. However, due to the epidemic and lockdown, sales had plummeted, and the future of the company was at risk.

Over a drink at the pub, Goodbody saw an opportunity. The Conservative government had started to open up the economy, and UK residents were having to travel, either for work, family, or much-needed holidays. The government had a list of approved clinics which could administer PCR tests to enable travellers to and from the UK to ascertain their COVID-free status.

Goodbody spotted a gap in the market—there were no guaranteed fast tests for people who had to fly out of the country at short notice. All the other private approved testers were at least 48-72 hours long and offered less-than-ideal customer service.

They had no expertise in the area, but they did have a crucial advantage—a network of independent pharmacies across the country with available consultation rooms and highly trained staff with expertise on COVID who were readily available on the high street. Studies had shown that the community pharmacist was one of the most trusted healthcare professionals on the UK high street.[24]

---

24 https://psnc.org.uk/services-commissioning/essential-facts-stats-and-quotes-relating-to-pharmacy-and-phar-macy-professionals/

So Goodbody pivoted. And what a pivot it was. From one of the first cannabinoid substances providers (CBD) to a leader in PCR and antigen COVID tests. And after months of careful planning, success followed.

And I know.

Because I was part of that initial pilot to validate the scheme in my city of Plymouth. As a consultant pharmacist, I worked with them to roll it out in the local pharmacy I had been contracted to work in during the COVID epidemic. As I met the COO, I was struck by the humility and the clarity of his pitch. He had clearly birthed and validated the concept.

Just three months later, Goodbody was making up to £7,000.00 per day, per pharmacy in the UK, and they had signed up more than 60 (and counting) independent pharmacies across England and Wales. The network is quickly growing by the day, and more importantly, not one patient has had to miss a flight because they failed to get their PCR results on time. They made $17 million in revenue in 2021, which was EIGHT times what they made in 2020 due to this simple but carefully planned, birthed, and executed pivot. [25]

The vision of great customer service of Goodbody had stayed the same, but the mode of delivery had changed. We talk more about this when we look at validation in more detail in part two of the book under the section on pain.

VALIDATION BY AFFIRMATION

Surround yourself with people that change how you think
Not people that nod their head and act like they agree...
...Cut out the lies stay close to people you know are loyal,
Grab your own glass and fill it
Don't let your fear destroy you, woo!

- NF, "Remember This," *Perception*, 2020

---

25   https://uk.advfn.com/stock-market/AQSE/goodbody-health-GDBY/share-news/
Goodbody-Health-Inc-Strong-2021-revenue-continuin/87510510

If you believe in your idea, then there should be no fear to sell it to carefully chosen colleagues, experts, potential customers, investors, and perhaps most of all, yourself.

Despite the severe setbacks I faced in the process of launching BlueCloud, I have never lost faith in the idea. That is because I experienced profound validation when giving talks and leading discussions at conferences in Geneva, London, Cape Town, Luanda, Coventry, and Accra. No matter where I was, the results have always been the same. Not one single audience has doubted the validity of the idea itself, its potential impact, and whether it would work. The feedback on the idea has always been positive, no matter where I have delivered it.

The lack of take-off has always come from other issues, which I will describe candidly later in the book. But not the basic idea or how to deliver it. And there is a kind of feedback that takes place with positive reinforcement. The more you pitch your idea, the better you become at it, the more refined the idea becomes, and the more convinced you are of its eventual success. But the reverse is also true. If the feedback is consistently negative, then this may be an indication that the idea is flawed and may need revisiting or complete overhauling.

Not quitting, or giving up, but *pivoting*, and in the meantime just waiting, waiting, waiting for the right time, the right moment.

VALIDATION BY BEGINNING WITH THE END IN MIND

When you lead me on
With your pseudo sun
Your light might not be all that bright
But in the dark it feels so strong
I am the moth beating his wings against the dusty window
Outside of your dull, fluorescent light
And my wings can't last this long…

- Switchfoot, "Fluorescent," *Interrobang*, 2021

Switchfoot, an American, Grammy-Award-winning rock band from San Diego, California are one of my favourite rock bands of all time. Their honest lyrics and energetic live shows have been a mainstay of dedicated fans from South Africa to Philippines, from Britain to the United States.

Their lyrics feature prominently in my journals and loudly on the kitchen JBL stereo speaker, much to the annoyance of my family.

This song, which only came out last week as I write, reminded me of my days as a child in Accra, Ghana.

We had fluorescent lights which came on at night at home, as was the case then throughout the country, and I used to stand for hours watching as moths, crickets, and other insects were attracted to their flickering, bright radiation.

But any fault in the bulb, or in the electricity supply, or connections to the mains, meant that the lights would flicker, flicker, and sometimes finally go dead, plunging us into total darkness—where we had to go scrambling for kerosene-fuelled lanterns to keep the lights on.

It occurred to me that our ideas are much the same.

By reinforcing the validation of your idea, using the means detailed above, you are building a clear picture of the business that remains illuminated, much like a fluorescent light in your mind. While this light may flicker, flicker, especially in the dark times, it should never go dead.

Never.

For it is this, and this alone, the picture of the final business in your head, the light in the distance, that will keep hope alive in the dark days. And it might just be the difference between success and failure.

VALIDATION BY PASSING THE FOUR PILLARS ETHICAL TEST

On January 16, 2015, David Hagenbuch, a writer with *Entrepreneur* magazine, wrote a poignant article on the four pillars of ethical enterprises. They are fairness, integrity, decency, and sustainability.

He says:

> Most people don't start a business thinking they're going to do the wrong thing. However, ethical challenges inevitably arise. **It's even more difficult to do the right thing if your company is not anchored from the onset to a strong moral base.** Entrepreneurs can lay a firm ethical foundation for their enterprise by ensuring a "yes" to these four crucial questions:

> 1. **Fairness: Is your business model based on win-win outcomes for both company and consumer?** A core tenet of any ethical business is that both company and consumer should come out ahead. A need to win at your customer's expense is a fundamental moral lapse.

> 2. **Integrity: Can your business's products/services be promoted with the truth?** Creativity in communication is a good thing, but a need to change the truth is a clear sign of a morally flawed foundation.

> 3. **Decency: Can you unashamedly tell others what your business does?** You should be able to describe with pride your business to your spouse, children, father, and everyone else. Embarrassment may indicate a morally suspect business model.

> 4. **Sustainability: Does your business make efficient use of resources?** This implies practicing good stewardship of resources to support the long-term wellbeing of everyone, not just primary stakeholders. **A business model based on reckless consumption is not only inefficient but is ethically irresponsible** (emphasis mine).[26]

---

26 https://www.entrepreneur.com/article/240035

I have put this as a last and final validation test because in my view, these four pillars should be a foundation for ethical entrepreneurship. They provide a frame of reference and a stable foundation.

We'll return to the concept of validation later in the book when we address the issue of pain in entrepreneurship.

KEY CONCEPTS:
- The Camel Principle
- The six types of validation
- The four pillars test

QUESTIONS:
1. Where are you on your journey of validation?

2. What do you currently have, and what do you need to be able to move through the Formative Period?

THE PASSION

The Passion

Stay for me there, stay for me
So the world becomes a prayer
A vast precious jewel
You
the crystal light of life here
dissolves
shimmering in its last ecstasy
of long day dawn triumph of pain
on this brink…..

- Kofi Awoonor, "Love," *The Promise of Hope,* 2014

I remember it well.

I was alone.

It was 4:30 a.m. and pitch black as I sat alone on my sofa.

I was literally penniless, £60,000 in debt, embroiled in toxic business relationships, and riddled with humiliating sickness and moral failure.

There were stacks of letters from credit card companies, the Inland Revenue Service, utility companies, and bills left unpaid. This did not include the tens of thousands of pounds owed to my close family and friends.

Few of my partners at the time were willing to take my calls, answer my texts, or respond to my emails.

I was alone.

Tears were running down my eyes.

The company I had formed with so much promise was dead in the water.

I had to bite the bullet and make the call to friends and family for even more—for a rudder to steer myself out of this mess.

And even that wasn't enough.

The next step was a bankruptcy call and a debt repayment scheme that was to last for the best part of a decade.

The thing I loved most was also responsible for my business death.

It was all I had left, and on that dark morning, it put its arms around me and kept me company. It refused to leave. Like Marmite, or British Rapper Little Simz's 2021 hit (which had just been released as I write this), "I Love You, I Hate You," I loved and hated it at the same time. It's funny how a song could so completely and accurately reflect how I felt that morning, but large chunks of the lyrics of that song did exactly that... I loved it and hated it at the exact same time.

It was called passion.

It's that indescribable force that moves you through life. It's that woozy immeasurable that captures your imagination and lifts you up in the face of grave disappointments and trials.

It is irrational. It cannot be measured, modelled, or put in a box and placed on the shelf. But you know when you have it, and you know when it's gone.

This book is not a discourse about the origins of passion. I don't know why some people are passionate about what they do. But I do know that it exists.

It's vital for your love life, your career, your business, your progress. Not only for you, but for the people around you. Your team, family, friends, colleagues. It's the fuel that keeps the car going.

The pursuit of an overriding purpose begins with passion. Passion is like the foundation for a home—it must be strong enough to support something lasting.

Passion is not denial. Passion doesn't pretend there are no obstacles, problems or difficulties.

The cyclist Davide Rebellin, who is still at the top of his game at 50 years old, cites passion as his driving force.

You are the only person who knows what you are passionate about. Just you.

Passion builds persistence. Persistence builds progress, and progress builds power.

I am unashamedly passionate about Africa.

As billionaire Aliko Dangote said, "Passion is what drives me forward. Passion is what makes me go to bed at two a.m. and wake up at six a.m."[27]

I am proudly African. I love the continent and have lived most of my life there. And yeah, I get it. The corruption, the rot, the poverty, the endless cycle of despondency, the bad press, the indescribable suffering and despair. African countries are rooted at the bottom of every statistic there is.

But wherever I travel, from Nigeria to Angola, from South Africa to Botswana, I see a resilience, a joy, opportunities wherever I look, and a people determined to make the best of their lives. It's a far cry from the press Africa gets when I am watching the news on BBC or CNN.

---

27 https://quotefancy.com/quote/1666807/Aliko-Dangote-Passion-is-what-drives-me-forward-Passion-is-what-makes-me-go-to-bed-at-2am

I am happiest, most fulfilled, when I am talking about Africa, when I am in Africa, or when I have closed a deal in Africa.

It doesn't matter that we have lost tens of thousands of pounds, and it has put me through some of my most harrowing experiences. It doesn't matter that the frustration of working and living there has driven me to the brink of despair, depression, and bankruptcy. The passion keeps picking me up, dusting me down, and placing me again in the thick of the boxing ring.

But passion by itself is not enough to ensure success, at least in the ethical sense. And that's why I have included it as one part, however crucial, of the Honeymoon Period. The person, the purpose, and the passion make it work, in that order.

Like fuel, passion can run out, and if it runs out, you're finished. So I have a few thoughts to share on how to keep that fuel in the car topped up, to ensure you can get to the destination. How? By celebrating the early wins, running with your kind, staying uncomfortable, and finding your fan.

So, let's dive in!

CELEBRATE THE EARLY WINS

I'm a winner, I'm a winner
Just believe that I'm a winner (I say just believe oh)
I will never do it like you do it
Just believe I'ma do it, do it
Allow me to enjoy myself

Allow me to enjoy myself
Allow me to enjoy myself
Allow me to enjoy myself

- Tekno Miles, "Enjoy," *Old Romance,* 2020

"Enjoy," the song by Nigerian Afrobeat superstar Tekno Miles, is a staple song enjoyed at parties in the West African Anglophone community. It's a song with uplifting beats and soaring lyrics that sends partying Africans into realms of dance and laughter. I'm listening to it as I write this. I love it.

And for some reason, it reminds me of when we signed our first deal in Lagos, Nigeria. That evening, we went out to party. And party we did. It still brings smiles to me, now as I recall hot chilli kebabs and glasses of shandy and beer in a penthouse restaurant with Indians, Angolans, Portuguese, Nigerians, and British. We had flown from all over the world to close the deal. It had taken months of painstaking work, but it was done. And it was a night to celebrate.

Years later, even though that deal brought us lots of pain (I talk more about that later), I still remember that night. And I'm glad we celebrated it like we did.

Because that deal now is worth millions of dollars and has brought untold benefits in health to hundreds of thousands of Africans. But every time I think of that deal and the pain it brought us later, I remember that night in that Lagos penthouse restaurant.

Celebrate the early wins. Take pictures. Write the dates down in your diary. Like my wife Dela did last night when she lost three kilos in the first three days in her quest to regain her fitness by following the 800-calorie diet after she was hit by COVID. You will need it when the times get tough, believe me.

RUN WITH YOUR KIND

According to you,
People like me
Shouldn't go into places like this or
Be around people like these.
But you don't know the half of it....

- Yrsa Daley-Ward, "You Don't Know the Half of It," *Bone,* 2017

Over the years, I have formed strong links with fellow African entrepreneurs. From Kojo Parris, an alumnus of Oxford and starter of the 2 Billion Rand Fund in Cape Town, to Chibuzo Opara, head of DrugStoc in Nigeria, to Oz Nieto, entrepreneur in logistics and agribusiness in Angola, and Mrs. Patience Tsegah, head of Unicom, one of Ghana's biggest pharmaceutical wholesalers.

They keep me inspired by their passion, grounded in reality.

Paradoxically, I have maintained minimum contact with most diasporan professional Africans here in the West who are typically professionals and consultants working for big firms. Their stories of corruption and hopelessness in Africa, fuelled by speculation, bad press from major Western news outlets, and returning professionals who only spent 2 to 3 weeks on holiday.

They kept me depressed by their pessimism, grounded in reality.

So, like a child on a swing in a park, I oscillated between hope in the future of the dark continent and hopelessness about the fate of the dark continent.

Until one day, I made a scientific and reasonable decision. It was the same kind of decision that saved my marriage, and the principle behind it governs algorithms for all social media platforms. What you feed grows bigger. What you starve will eventually die.

You cannot constantly hear negativity without having some of it rub off on you, bestselling author Charles Swindoll says.[28] If you are prone to discouragement, you can't run the risk of spending a lot of your time with people who traffic in discouraging information.

I decided to spend time with the Africans who were actually on the ground, moving the continent forward. These are Africans who had

---

28 Swindoll, Charles, Hand me another brick: Building Character in Yourself and Others (TN, Nashville, Bantam Books, 1978)

lived, learned, and worked in the West, but still opted to go back to start their businesses. I say this, of course, whilst recognising the validity of my fellow diasporans.

Guy Raz talks about the difference between dangerous and scary and makes the point that we are more relaxed around things we are more acquainted with. Fundamentally, he adds, "Entrepreneurs were taking the detour—the leap—away from the type of professional life they didn't want and toward something new and exciting, and their own."[29]

Yes, just like starting a new business in uncertain terrain, Africa is scary, but not dangerous.

So I decided to go with the guys on the ground. And they have kept my fuel topped up, even after 12 years of trying and failing and finally succeeding.

STAY UNCOMFORTABLE

Truth is a beauty, whether pretty or not.
Love doesn't mean you should stay
Sometimes, the truth has to punch you, twice.
Love doesn't always mean you should stay.
Love is not a safe word
But it's the safe things that kill you in the end.

- Yrsa Daley-Ward, "Things It Can Take Twenty Years and a Bad Liver to Work Out," *Bone*, 2017

Steve Harvey, American television and radio presenter, as well as actor, author and philanthropist, made a great point about staying uncomfortable:

---

29 Raz, Guy, Ibid.

"If you stay in your comfort zone, that's where you will fail. You will fail in your comfort zone. Success is a very uncomfortable procedure. It is a very uncomfortable thing to attempt. Start putting some pressure on yourself."[30]

When I was eight years old, in the midst of the Cold War, I remember winning a book as a prize in school for academic achievement in science.

Africa in those days was informed by the fight between the USSR and the USA for dominance. We had seen its devastating impact two doors away, in neighbouring Nigeria with the Biafran War. The USSR supported the breakaway hopeful Biafra nation, whilst the US supported the Nigerian government. That war caused great grief, cost thousands of lives, and left scars which are still visible in the Delta region of Nigeria today.

The book was about the space travel from a Russian perspective. And it was surprisingly conciliatory towards the Americans, which is one reason I remember it decades later. The book is called *The Sun's Wind*, by Alexei Leonov.[31]

It was in that book that I learnt about the incredible energy needed for the Russian spacecraft Soyuz to escape the earth's gravitational pull. I also learned about how much research, collaboration, money, and time had been spent in accomplishing this singular feat.

But like Soyuz, it takes an inhumane amount of energy, effort and courage to leave you safe zone to follow your passion.

And like Soyuz, I needed the energy to break out of the comfort zone of my 9-5 planet.

This discomfort has come from 15 years of trying to break out of the gravitational pull of the middle class. I have seen scores of people try and fail, only to end up being pulled back in the fold of the middle.

---

30 https://steveharvey.com/get-comfortable-being-uncomfortable/ Harveys, Hundreds – Get Comfortable Being Uncomfortable
31 Leonov, Alexei, The Sun's Wind (Moscow, Progress Publishers, 1977)

That has burned so much into my psyche that I unconsciously seek out and support people who are the same.

It's exemplified by this book and in particular by all the artists, countries, musicians, books and poets you've probably never heard of. Their stories, music and poems inspire me to no end. And I think part of my life's purpose will be to help them to break out into the mainstream in any small way I can.

Like the rapper NF.

I have been following NF since 2014. I absolutely love his music, and it was always on full blast in my earbuds on my early-morning run for over seven years. I was, and still am, a devoted fan.

He finally entered the mainstream after years of recording with his breakout single "Let You Down" from the album *Perception* that took the hip-hop world by storm and peaked at number one on the Billboard 200. He's never looked back since. Finally, after years of trying, he succeeded in escaping the gravitational pull of the middle. I jumped and pumped my fists at the news. And it turns out this wasn't a fluke.

Two years later, the album *Search* did even better.

My amusement was at the mainstream media, who had never heard of him, and the assumption that he came out of nowhere.

USA Today put it like this in its article from the 28th of October, 2019:

> In what may be a surprise to many music fans, the new album by Chance the Rapper, beloved *The Big Day*, was edged out of the No. 1 spot Billboard Top 200 Billboard Chart this week. What's likely an even bigger surprise is who beat him out. Meet a rapper with a much lower profile than Chance's, NF, with a devoted fanbase that propelled his release *The Search* to the top of the charts. Mainstream hip-hop fans might not understand how NF's *The Search*, which had no significant

media push around it, topped *The Big Day*, an album that saw Chance partnering with Lyft and giving major interviews in support of the release.

But NF is no stranger to the top of the charts, and while Chance's first-week success for *The Big Day* was largely driven by streaming, NF's fans flocked to the iTunes store to buy the album, with traditional sales driving his big numbers for *The Search*. [32]

The odds were stacked against him. He's white in a genre dominated by black artists. He signed up to the only record label that would take him on, a little-known Christian label which brought him much controversy. He doesn't swear or use vulgar language on any of his tracks. And he doesn't talk about sex, drugs, or violence. And he had no money and little publicity.

And he is one reason why I think there is always a chance for underdogs like us.

And he did it by staying uncomfortable.

With his label—pigeonholed as a Christian artist.

With his life—an absent mother who died from a drug overdose and an abusive father. This discomfort goes right through his music right from the album *Mansion* in 2015 to *Clouds* in 2021. You can feel it in his lyrics.

And it finally paid off.

And if it happened to NF with *Perception,* though he was virtually unknown, your new service or product going out there and completely disrupting, hammering, and taking over your niche of the market, or even this book going out to be a Sunday Times Best Seller.

---

32 https://eu.usatoday.com/story/entertainment/music/2019/08/06/
 who-nf-eminem-soundalike-who-beat-chance-rapper-no-1-album/1935006001/

You never know.

Author and researcher Peter Hollins, in his book, *Finish What You Start*, talks about the mindset of comfort with discomfort.

He writes:

> A critical mindset is believing that your journey to success will become supremely uncomfortable at times, so you need to get comfortable with discomfort....to be successful and never give up, you need to minimise negative consequences of uncomfortable situations by getting immunised to the sense of discomfort.[33]

There is no shortcut to staying uncomfortable. You have to continually put yourself out there. Keep putting pressure on yourself.

There is a term that is being bandied about a lot these days.

The impostor syndrome.

But, you ask, what has that got to do with passion?

Everything.

Growth is an incredibly important fuel of passion—being motivated, fulfilled and happy. But if you are ever going to grow, you have to change gears, change rooms, change positions, take that one step outside your comfort zone. And each time you do that, you will feel incapable, like you're winging it.

So if you're to grow, to top up your passion, you should feel like you're an impostor. You should feel uncomfortable. That is a sure sign that you're in the right zone and is the only sign that you're progressing.

---

33 Hollins, Peter. *Finish What you Start- The Art of Following Through, Taking Action, Executing & Self Discipline* (USA, 2018)

Steven Bartlett, *Dragon's Den* judge, entrepreneur, and the CEO of Social Chain, talked about this:

> In my whole life I have tried to escape my zone of comfort and keeping myself one foot out of that zone of comfort—and when you do that, the zone of comfort expands—you take one more step, and you take one more step and it expands to match…if you want to spend your time growing, and progressing, and thereby being fulfilled, you should always feel like an impostor…if you're not feeling that way, then maybe you're playing it too safe—not challenging yourself enough.[34]

I remember seeing him for the first day on *Dragon's Den*. A 29-year-old black man, who grew up in one of the poorest parts of my native adopted city of Plymouth —he looked out of place.

But he has proved himself that he deserves a seat at that table. 100 percent.

While there is no progress without passion, finding the right balance is crucial. Enough to stay uncomfortable, but not too much to burn out.

I remember when I had an invitation to be inducted into the African Leaders Hall of Fame by the *African Leadership* magazine.

I felt like an impostor. I felt uncomfortable, like I didn't belong.

But as I posted it on LinkedIn and had thousands of likes, approvals and cheers, I thought to myself, *Maybe I do belong here.*

I could feel the fuel in my tank being topped up.

I had thrown my hat into the ring.

And I really hope you do so too, with some encouragement, and a few diehard fans cheering you on.

---

34 https://www.facebook.com/watch/?v=4943114739069788

FIND YOUR FAN

I wanna be there when the voices in your head
Are loud enough to make you lose your mind
Just the same when you're dominating the day
I wanna be the one who's by your side
You know my love is not the jealous type
It doesn't matter if we win or lose
I could stay or I could come no matter where you're coming from
I could be the one to let you choose

I wanna hold you close but never hold you back
Just like the banks to the river
And if you ever feel like you're not enough
I'm gonna break all your mirrors
I wanna be there when the darkness closes in
To make the truth a little clearer
I wanna hold you close but never hold you back
I'll be the banks for your river

- NEEDTOBREATHE, "Banks," *Out of Body,* 2020

I hated the coal pot.

It was a sturdy metal contraption with a wide top for storing charcoal and a base for collecting the ash which was used and is still used for cooking in Western Sub-Saharan Africa.

Because of the irregular supply of electricity in my young days in Ghana, West Africa, my mother used to cook all our meals on coal pots, the rough equivalent of our barbecues here in the West. But unlike here, the coal pot was a daily occurrence, not just out at summer or during parties in the garden, or at get-togethers on the beach.

But the procedure was the same.

1. Get the coal pot out from the shed

2. Fill it with charcoal

3. Pour kerosene, light a match, and then fan the flame with a specially made knitted fan till the charcoal lapped up the fire and became red

4. Then cook.

My job as a child was to grab a stool and fan the flame like crazy till the charcoal became red hot. With time, the embers turned to ash, which collected at the base. My mom would then have to refill the coal pot with more charcoal, and then I would have to repeat the process.

Being disorganised, as I was then, I could never find the fan because I never returned it to its allocated place after using it. So I had to endure my mother shouting how careless I was and repeatedly asking why I didn't just put the fan where it was meant to go after the food was cooked.

I heaved a sigh of relief when the food was finally cooked and left to warm. Then I could finally rush out to play football with my friends in the sand and sun-drenched sky without the fear of being called in again to fan the flames—forgetting once again to put the fan in its allocated spot.

To keep your passion topped up, you need to find your fan. Your biggest fan, the one person who is cheering your corner. They believe in you, remind you of your worth, goad and coax you, and fan the flames of your passion when you are embers burning out.

Their cheering voices can still resound in your head even after they've gone.

I would have given up long ago if I didn't have few fans cheering in my corner.

My "armour-bearing," longsuffering mate, as he likes to put it, of two decades—Brian Martin.

Our family friend Kate Wright, who encouraged me, believed in me, and cheered me on when everything looked bleak.

My brother Michael, who bankrolled me when I was penniless, broke, and on the verge of giving up.

My daughter Nshira, who quietly, consistently believed in me in a way that only a 12-year-old could. I was determined not to let her down.

I will talk about loneliness later on, but without Brian, Michael, Kate, and Nshira, it's fair to say I probably would have thrown in the towel. I wouldn't have coped.

So, make sure you find your fan.

Or fans. There's at least one for every entrepreneur.

And once you find your fan, don't keep losing it, like I kept losing mine when fanning mother's coal pot. Guard your fan(s) and keep them for dear life.

They might just be the difference between success… and failure.

And I don't need to tell you the criteria for what your fan should look like. Grammy-award-nominated band NEEDTOBREATHE has already done it for me. Check out the lyrics of their song at the beginning of this section.

"Banks."

SUMMARY OF THE HONEYMOON PERIOD:

So, to reiterate, the Honeymoon Period consists of the holy trinity: the person, the purpose, and the passion.

The Person: it is vital to "start with who," which means getting your principles and WGLL straight. You want to know you are in the right car for the journey.

The Purpose: it is vital to start with your "why" well researched, recorded, and validated, such that you have a clear sense that the car is headed toward a good and worthy destination.

The Passion: And finally, you must have the fuel in the car to take you to that destination.

Once we have these sealed up, and we've imbibed the Camel Principle, then, and only then, are we ready to pack bag and baggage, pick up the keys, and ride into the sunset to face the next part of the journey—the wilderness of entrepreneurship—a battlefield where many lose their mojo and many find it.

Have you got what it takes?

I believe you do, or you wouldn't have picked up this book.

The next phase of the journey.

The Formative Period.

KEY CONCEPTS:
- Celebrating the early wins
- Surrounding yourself with the right people
- Pushing your limits and staying uncomfortable
- Finding your fans or supporters

QUESTIONS:
1. How do you experience your passion?

2. Take a moment to reflect on the people you surround yourself with. Who are they, and what kinds of messages do they send you about your work as an entrepreneur? What does your comfort zone look like? Where could you be edging more into discomfort?

3. Create a list of your fans. Is there more you can do to cultivate this for yourself?

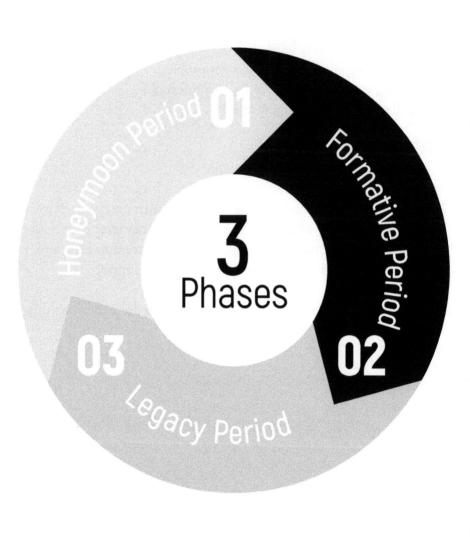

THE FORMATIVE PERIOD

**"I am the tall dark stranger
Those warnings prepared you for"**

Yrsa Daley-Ward, "Intro," Bone, 2017

Attention please!
May I have your attention please!
Will the real Ethical Entrepreneur stand up?
I repeat, will the real ethical entrepreneur stand up?
Are we gonna have a problem here? [35]

The Formative Period of entrepreneurship follows the Honeymoon. It is where success and failure are defined. It is where you grow up and begin to use the fat of the Camel Principle. The Formative Period separates the men from the boys—it's the filter where the real entrepreneur stands up and fights for what they believe in, what they have nursed over the Honeymoon Period.

---

[35] This is a play on Eminem's 'The Real Slim Shady' hit of 2000.

It's where you go out into the public, where you face the pain, the payoff, the price. It's where you must build your discipline and develop your thick skin. It's where nature tests your resolve.

But it's also the place of hope and strength because it is at this phase that you may get to meet your partner, where your purpose is validated, where you prepare for success. Real success.

But let's get the meatier bits out of the way first. Let's clear the path by dealing with what all entrepreneurs must face to one degree or the other.

Pain.

THE PAIN

Pain!
You made me a
You made a believer, believer
Pain!
You break me down and build me up believer, believer
Pain!

Oh, let the bullets fly, oh, let them rain
My life, my love, it came from...
Pain!
You made me a
You made me a believer, believer

- Imagine Dragons, "Believer," *Evolve,* 2017

Pain in building a business is well documented, but yes, that's it. Documented. There is the insistence that yes it exists, yes you will have to struggle, but if you make it through the pain, if you keep going, and treat it as part of the learning cycle, you'll make it.

But is this completely true?

Obviously, if 90 percent of businesses are failing after 10 years, as we've seen in the introduction, then the pain of carrying on was too much to bear, so evidently, closing down was deemed easier than soldiering on.

I think the problem may be the fact that pain is hard to quantify, put in a box, and explain away. Behind the statistics of failure lie some really heart-breaking stories, and the plethora of books that have been written have not moved the needle in terms of success.

But after 10 years of trying, rejection, and going through pain of all sorts, I am going here to attempt to do the near impossible—to build a pain model.

Why is it almost impossible? Because in the heat of it, pain is hard to quantify. It manifests in the same way—regardless of the source. I can sometimes feel it like a cut—a sickle-shaped wound just below the crevices of my heart. Sometimes, I feel like I could almost point to it. And I—no, we—as entrepreneurs, businesspeople, leaders, are sometimes so focused in making it go away that we don't spend enough time to reflect on its source, its origins, its pathways, and, in so doing, get the right ways to deal with it.

But how do we deal with pain? How do we look beyond whatever we are going through now to the other side?

Certainly by **not** being forced to 'smile and wave.'

Or, as it's commonly called, toxic positivity.

Wharton Professor and multiple bestselling author Adam Grant elaborates:

> Toxic Positivity is pressuring people to look on the bright side. They have to suppress anxiety, anger, sadness, and grief.
>
> {**However**} healthy support is shielding people from the dark side. You invite them to express their pain and show them they're not alone and won't feel it forever.[36]

And this, my dear readers, is exactly what I'd like to do here.

As I write this, Simone Biles, the US Olympian who was famous in Rio 2016, has pulled out many of her main events for Tokyo 2020, citing mental struggles. This would have been unthinkable just a decade ago—she would have been told to just 'get on with it.'

---

36 Quote on Twitter: @AdamMGrant https://twitter.com/AdamMGrant/status/1510258444657377285

And in going through over 20 years of my own journaling, where I describe a number of different types of pain, as well as listening to fellow struggling entrepreneurs, with help along the way from literature, music, and other forms of art, I have come to the conclusion that a model of pain is not only possible, but necessary.

But this model will only work if we focus on the response to the pain, without trying to ask the why or question the fairness.

Because the plain truth of the matter is that life is not fair.

The sooner we understand this, let it sink into our psyche and roll with it, the easier our paths will be.

Life is not fair.

We can't always choose what will happen to us (though, as you will read in the model to follow, a lot of our pain is due to our own decisions), but we can definitely choose our response. And it is our response that will, in large part, determine where we go from here.

Now, again to emphasise: this is not to minimise the pain, to explain it away, to find reasons for it. In the past and even now, a lot of famous businessmen, successful entrepreneurs, and famous celebrities have gone through unimaginable losses, and it's only in the last five years or so that people are beginning to appreciate that coming out and talking about your pain and struggle is not a sign of weakness, but rather a sign of strength.

But we have a chance to beat it, overcome it, manage it and even turn it to our advantage. If our foundations (AKA the Honeymoon Period) are strong, then we have every chance of making it through these trials.

But we need to be realistic. As I said earlier, like a scar after a wound, pain never goes away completely.

We just get better at managing it, dealing with it, and turning it towards our advantage.

Much like climbing a huge house with stairs and a twisting banister and looking down, we will come to the same source of the pain, again and again, but hopefully from a higher angle and better focus, looking down on it with greater breadth and depth of understanding from a higher and higher level, saying, "Aha! I've seen you before! And you're not going to get me this time, no way!"

To make this work, I have decided to be candid about my own pain. It's going to come as shock to many who know me, maybe not the pain itself, but the response to the pain.

And that is what the model will be based on. Not the pain, but the response to the pain.

I have called it the Pain Flag Response Model.

For me, pain in building a business comes from four primary sources. I've categorized these forms of pain and the corresponding responses with four colours: Red, White, Amber, and Green. The model is shown in the diagram below:

RED FLAG PAIN

THE PAIN OF SELF-SABOTAGE—STOP

15 March, 2013

> *See, nobody warns you about yourself*
> *The red in your eye*
> *The trap in your mouth*
>
> *The person who hurts you the most in the end will be you*
> *Almost every time, you.*
>
> *You'd better learn to forgive yourself*
> *Forgive yourself instantly*
> *It's a skill you're going to need until you die.*
>
> - Yrsa Daley-Ward, "Things It Can Take Twenty Years and a Bad Liver to Work Out," *Bone,* (2017)

I sat on the bed, crying with frustration, deep pain, and, yes, hopelessness.

And the culprit?

Pornography.

The rejection I had faced since I was a boy was resurfacing with the rejection of deals related to BlueCloud. By that point, it had happened over 150 times, and it had taken its toll.

I felt worthless.

I had taken a sneak peek once, a few years ago. Then two, then three.

Since then, it had completely taken over my life. Every spare moment I could find, every little breather. I had a full-blown addiction.

I saw my whole life falling around me like a Ponzi scheme, a house of cards. I was in big, big trouble.

The chickens had come home to roost.

My family and close friends found out. To say they were upset would have been an understatement. But they were gracious to me. I got off with a warning. I wish I could say that was the last time. Not a chance.

10 March, 2016

I had managed to go three years clean, and was feeling proud of myself. Very smug.

But like a bad penny, the addiction bounced back.

I remember it well.

It started on a high—we had just signed an MOU for a $16-million healthcare diagnostic deal in Southern Africa.

The temptation was so bad that day, on the hotel bed in Lagos, Nigeria, that I gave in. I thought just this once wouldn't hurt.

But, oh boy, did it hurt.

Six months later, the addiction was back in full swing.

I remember that night when I cried out in desperation. I felt completely worthless, hopeless, like a piece of trash. Up till then, Dela hadn't found out. But I knew it was only a matter of time. She was a smart girl. She would see the signs.

A search on the internet for help came up with a unique software tool.

It was called Covenant Eyes.

I signed up and followed its instructions. It recommended accountability partners, downloading its software onto all your devices, and regular updates as well as regular conversations.

It promised results, but with a good dose of tough love. But I knew I had to cut the crap once and for all. I was leading a double life.

2021, close to £1000 later and lots of clampdowns and honest conversations, and I'm still clean. But I caused so much pain, so much hurt, and developed bad habits that nearly cost me everything.

This is the pain I have called Red Flag Pain. It's the pain caused almost exclusively by our bad decisions, habits, and hang-ups. It's a response that acts like a false crutch for a deep recurring pain —but that crutch never lasts. It's a false promise, a phantom solution, like a spray from an aerosol, here one moment, gone the next. And often those closest to us are left unfairly having to pick up the messy pieces we leave behind.

Red Flag Pain is the simplest and easiest to diagnose, but it's incredibly difficult to fix.

And it's called a red flag because even though it may be difficult to fix, the solution is incredibly simple and can be encapsulated in a single word:

STOP

That's it. Stop. HALT. Get help. Do what you must, but as the Grammy-nominated, double-platinum-selling rock band Skillet says:

"No one can make it better,
Take control, it's now or never
If you're sick of it, get rid of it!"

In my case, it was an accountability partner, Covenant Eyes, and a watchful and loving partner. That's right. I had to come clean to her. I could see the pain I had caused. But she forgave me. I didn't deserve to be forgiven, but I knew when I had to stop. Right at the tip of the red light. Going any further would have resulted in a huge crash. Like Fela.

Fela Aníkúlápó Kuti did not know when to stop. He married 12 wives and divorced them all as well. He was notorious for his impulsive, extreme sexist behaviour, sexual impropriety, and volatile temper. The warning signs were obvious. His influence and music quality waned more and more as his outrageous behaviour grew in proportion. He finally died, allegedly from AIDS complications, and his legacy, though great, would have been exponential if he had heeded the warnings, the numerous red lights.

He paid the consequences with his life, and his legacy suffered as a result. Whenever people think about reggae, they think Bob Marley. But very few people associate Afrobeat with Fela, even though he can justifiably claim to be the originator of African Afrobeat, which has now produced worldwide sensations like Burna Boy, Shatta Wale, Wizkid, and Davido.

His name, Aníkúlápó, literally means *'one who carries death in his pouch.'*

He refused to stop at the red light. He self-sabotaged.

We are no different from all the famous ones before us who have wrecked their careers with alcohol and drug abuse, mistreating of spouses, or the one million other bad habits we know will wreck us, but still continue to do anyway.

As award-winning poet Kayo Chingonyi aptly puts it:

> *The nucleus of an infected cell*
> *Is a pathogen's ultimate gateway—*
> *After the breach, the sounding of a knell,*
> *The ending of a life, or so they say.*
> *I believed it too, to my great shame,*
> *As did my mother who refused the pills*
> *That would have her here among us still.*

- Kayo Chingonyi, "Viral," *A Blood Condition*, 2021

But even the more insidious ones are the bad habits that offend no one— not exercising, eating all the bad stuff. You know what yours is.

Correcting any problem begins by looking it squarely in the eye and facing it head on. It's so easy to take the philosophy of the song "Human" by rock musician Rag'n'Bone Man—"don't put your blame on me because I'm only human."

Yes, you're human. Just like all of us.

But that's the reason why you should deal with the Red Flag Pain before it completely derails you.

Deal with it. Don't dodge it. If you don't break it, it will break you.

But how do you deal with Red Flag Pain?

There are a plethora of support programmes, counsellors, coaches, and communities that deal with various aspects of Red Flag Pain, be it over-eating, alcoholism, or pornography. In my opinion, every support system must have six defining characteristics to ensure success:

1. Acceptance of the fact that there is a problem, that things need to change, and that help is needed **outside** the victim.

2. Things need to come out at least partially into the open. I was reminded of this a few years ago when my son swallowed a spider and some bleach. He was extremely unwell and was sick on our lovely carpet. But he felt better almost instantaneously after everything came out. (We did seek medical help immediately in case you're wondering.)

3. There **needs** to be accountability partners and a mechanism in place which provides checks for reoffending.

4. There should be an aspect of digging, preferably with counselling of some sort, to reveal *why* the Red Flag Pain arises in the first place and develop strategies to recognise the triggers for the pain.

5. There also needs to be a sort of non-judgemental support system in place.

6. Finally, there should be what I call a **reject and replace**; a firm commitment to not only stop the bad behaviour but replace it with an alternative good habit.

But Red Flag Pain is not all that there is—there are three other types of pain that can arise in the business journey:

WHITE FLAG PAIN

THE PAIN OF THE UNFAIRNESS OF LIFE—SURRENDER

I won't wave my white flag, no
This time I won't let go
I'd rather die
Than give up the fight, give up the fight
I won't wave my white flag, no
Oh I won't go down slow
I'd rather die
Than give up the fight, give up the fight

Smoke, fire, it's all going up
Don't you know I ain't afraid to shed a little blood
Smoke, fire, flares are going up, flares are going up

Oh I won't wave my white flag, no...

- Bishop Briggs, "White Flag," *Church of Scars*, 2018

We all have our white flags.

In the contours, journeys, and mazes of life, you come across ordinary people who lead extraordinary lives.

One such person is June Lawrence.

I worked with June for 10 years when I was a locum consultant pharmacist with a private pharmacy chain for the NHS.

She really is a remarkable woman.

Her former husband had abandoned her and left her with an only child. She remarried and, in the space of two years, lost everything.

She lost her father to cancer.

Then two years later, she lost her uncle, again, to cancer.

Then, a year later, she lost her husband to cancer.

And then, just last week, she lost her 52-year-old brother to cancer.

During the pandemic, she had to stay home to look after her ill husband, and as a result, she couldn't return to work. So she lost her job. She had worked that job for 28 years, serving the people of Stonehouse, Plymouth as a dispensing assistant, and had even been recognised in the local paper for her unselfish service.

And she left that job with not so much as a thank you from the company she had worked so hard for. And she had not had a pay rise in 15 of those 28 years.

She was one of the kindest, loveliest, and most unselfish people I had ever met.

I lost contact with June for a couple of years until the quote she always used to say came to my mind. I quoted it at the beginning of PART 1 of this book.

'You have to appreciate the good times, to understand the bad.'

And I have had my fair share of White Flag Pain—I have lost my only sister, my first niece, survived two car crashes where the cars have been written off because they were damaged beyond repair, been diagnosed with epilepsy, which has cost me substantial injuries in the past, and nearly lost my wife to COVID.

White Flag Pain is the kind of pain that happens to you from the blows of life. Pain that creeps up on you when you aren't looking.

The pain that caused Bernice to return to England when she was halfway through building her school in Ghana.

The pain that forced me to give up one of the things I loved most in life—driving a brand-new car with the windows down and the stereo up.

The pain that forced me to sleep rough at train stations after returning from business trips in the Middle East and Africa because I had missed the last train back home and all the hotels in Exeter and Paddington that I could afford were all fully booked.

But I have called it White Flag Pain because there is only one word for the response:

SURRENDER.

You surrender to the pain, but surrender doesn't mean you give up your dream or vision. You surrender to the painful reality that your dream may take longer, may be more difficult. And you have to pivot more, adapt more, become a bit more flexible.

As bestselling author Sara Collins advises, "Approach whatever that is in a spirit of acceptance, and you will build your *business,* brick by brick."[37]

Every so often, you come across extraordinary entrepreneurs who have done just that.

Take, for example, Tammy Mildren, founder of Tammy's Beads.

Tammy has been clinically diagnosed with 10 serious, potentially life-changing medical disorders ranging from autism, ME, hypermobility syndrome, brittle bones, dyspraxia, and functional neurological disorder involving non-epileptic seizures. These seizures do not respond to medication and can attack her without warning.

She takes over 10 different medicines to manage her conditions. I know her well. She used to be one of my patients when I worked as a pharmacist in the inner city of Plymouth.

Last May, she was found unconscious in the car park where she had been in the freezing cold for over 30 minutes. She had had a seizure whilst emptying her bins.

She nearly lost her life that day.

She was later diagnosed with COVID which also nearly killed her and left her with long COVID, which further deteriorated her memory and her speech.

She has been picked up by ambulances so many times that she is now very well known in the Accident and Emergency Ward of Derriford Hospital, Plymouth's main central hospital.

She is noticeably autistic, has suffered countless fractures, and struggles with ME.

---

37 https://www.egaschool.co.uk/1239/anna-interviews-author-sara-collins

But she is also a professional dancer, with a degree of art and dance from Plymouth University, and an entrepreneur with a financially thriving business, Tammy's Beads, which specialises in making beaded jewellery and Autism/SEN-friendly products.

She is the inventor of the fidget poppet, a device used by severely autistic children to relieve their stress.

I caught up with her on the bus last week.

Her vivacious personality, loud voice, and dancing blue eyes do not give the impression of someone who is in continuous pain.

She acknowledged the limitations of her conditions as we chatted side by side in the packed creaky bus that rainy morning, her noticeable drawl somewhat muffled by the effect of the medicines to numb the continual pain…

> Any day could be my last. I resolve to live every day with gratitude, joy, and give it my best shot. I may not be able to take my business to the level and potential due to my physical limitations, but I resolve to use my dancing, coaching, seminars, and business to inspire, to relieve, to make as big a difference as I can.

For her, success doesn't mean building a multi-million-dollar organisation. 99 percent of people with half the conditions that she's got are in a wheelchair and housebound, totally dependent on carers and social services.

But she's clenched her teeth, accepted her limitations, and is doing the best with what she's got—helping hundreds of autistic children and making good money in the process.

But success here depends on how well you've navigated the Honeymoon Period.

If you have gone through your Honeymoon Period well, you will have deep roots, a big camel's hump, and a good banker's overdraft. And this will see you through, so even if the unimaginable happens, your legacy will live on. We'll talk more about this in part three of the book on the Legacy Period.

And that's why I love Bishop Briggs's 2018 breakthrough album, *Church of Scars*.

I especially love the title. Because that's exactly what White Flag Pain is. The pain leaves scars, but you have the opportunity to let those scars church you, school you, mold you, to be bigger, better, stronger, and more resilient.

So, even though it's unfair, surrender to the pain, but never surrender the war.

As author Steven Pressfield says, in his book *The War of Art*:

> There seems no way to make the experiences easier, nor any method to eliminate the pain. The lessons can't be taught. The agony cannot be inoculated against. There are no shortcuts. The only way is through.[38]

The process is about pain. The lessons come the hard way.

I have battled with epilepsy for a decade, since my first car crash in 2012. I've had fits in the bathroom, the car, on the pavement whilst running or walking, and during meetings at work.

The reason for these seizures remains unexplained.

I've tried therapy, have been seen by some of the top consultants in the world, and have experimented with all the whys—medication, therapy, increased rest, diet. It subsides, recoils, but never disappears.

I have suffered numerous falls physically, but also mentally, and in my

---

38 Pressfield, Steven, The War of Art: Break Through the Blocks and Win Your Inner Creative Battles (New York, Black Irish Entertainment, 2002)

business dealings due to this White Flag Pain. It has threatened my identity, my dignity, and my core pride as a person. There's nothing worse than your employees seeing you rigid on the floor, contorted and foaming at the mouth. There's a humility that such diseases bring, that force you to rethink your life.

It is my White Flag Pain that gave birth to this book.

I took up cycling to meetings and work because I couldn't drive as a result of having been diagnosed with uncontrolled epilepsy.

I also use the bus and the train. As I mentioned above, the toughest decision for me was to give up driving, but it was on the bus that I met Tammy, who gave me the inspiration and impetus for this section of this book.

So, every time White Flag Pain strikes, and you're tempted to give up, remember Bishop Briggs's "White Flag."

White Flag Pain.

It's unfair. It's not your fault. But you can choose how you respond.

Victim or victor?

Your choice.

GREEN FLAG PAIN
THE PAIN OF THE OBSERVER—GO

When they ask you how you are
Don't say fearful. Narrow your eyes
And kiss your teeth but don't say afraid.
Wipe the blood from yourself
Don't tell them what went on when
The sun was busy in another street

...

If they ask you how you are
Don't say stolen. Don't say forgotten, passed over,
Ignored. Don't you dare say Orphan.
Don't say beaten by the system
Oppressed and disturbed.
And don't you dare say disappointed
Don't you dare say damaged
Smile.
Smile with all your teeth, even the rotting ones.
Even the rotting ones.

- Yrsa Daley-Ward, "When They Ask," *Bone*, 2017

I am the man in the middle.

I am middle-aged.

I am a middle-class professional.

I fall into the middle class as defined by the Office of National Statistics here in the UK.

I live in a middle-class suburb in a middle-class city in Middle England.

I was brought up in a middle-class country and suburb in Africa, Ghana, by middle-class parents.

My income from my middle-class profession falls squarely into the middle-class salary bracket.

Most of my friends are middle-class—doctors, pharmacists, teachers, clergymen.

I go to middle-class meetings with like-minded professionals

I hold middle-class parties in my middle-class, semi-detached house with its middle-sized garden, where we discuss middle-class problems, such as the tax we have to pay, good education for our children, and moan on about how we are the squeezed middle.

I am a man in the middle.

And the middle is characterised by one word: COMFORT.

It struck me the other day how this has become ingrained in my psyche. I even seek out middle pubs and restaurants when I'm going out to eat—not too cheap, not too expensive.

Part of the greatest pain I have faced in starting BlueCloud is breaking out of the middle. It reminds me of Alexei Leonov's book I quoted earlier.

The middle is my greatest friend—and my greatest enemy.

My greatest comfort and the source of my greatest discomfort.

It presents as the nagging feeling that yes, I've done well, but…

And I feel this tension a lot in the music I like.

Because of this discomfort I have always felt, I am drawn to music which seems to fall into the same category.

Bands in the middle.

They usually attract between 500,000 to 3,000,000 listeners monthly on platforms like Spotify.

And they are present in every genre imaginable, followed by an extremely loyal fan base, without having broken through into the mainstream.

One theme runs through their music: the struggle they face to break out. The frustration of doing the best they can while being stuck in the middle.

Like "Thrive" by Grammy-awarded band Switchfoot, "Art of Survival" by Bishop Briggs, "Knock" by Shad, or "30" by Aitch, they remind me of one of my favourite US presidents, Theodore Roosevelt and his famous quote:

> It is not the critic who counts; not the man who points out how the strong man stumbles, or where the doer of deeds could have done them better. The credit belongs to the man who is actually in the arena, whose face is marred by dust and sweat and blood; who strives valiantly; who errs, who comes short again and again, because there is no effort without error and shortcoming; but who does actually strive to do the deeds; who knows great enthusiasms, the great devotions;

who spends himself in a worthy cause; who at the best knows in the end the triumph of high achievement, and who at the worst, if he fails, at least fails while daring greatly, so that his place shall never be with those cold and timid souls who neither know victory nor defeat.[39]

And for me, this is the greatest pain I have encountered on this journey: the Green Flag Pain. Pain caused as a consequence of my reaction to the voices and action of other people and my own. And I spend a considerable amount of time here because this is where, in my opinion, the struggle is greatest. And it is the most painful because we perceive it to be inflicted on us by the people closest to us: our loved ones.

But for this, the response is in keeping with the green at a traffic light. You listen and pivot if you must, but you keep going.

I'd like to break this down further into subcategories, illustrated by several stories.

- **The Pain of Betrayal**
- **The PHD Pain (As We Say in Africa)**
- **The 'Caring' Pain**
- **The 'Get Out of Your Head' Pain**

THE PAIN OF BETRAYAL

I am expecting a lawsuit of $100,000.00 any day now, through no fault of my own.

It was 8:15 p.m. at Paddington Station, London, five years ago in 2017.

I sat down on the hard bench in the freezing cold, staring up at the train timetable monitor, head in my hands, contemplating my next move.

---

39 https://www.artofmanliness.com/citizenship-in-a-republic-by-theodore-roosevelt/

All my best laid plans had been derailed by a 15-minute delay in the flight from Dubai to Heathrow.

I had missed the last train from Paddington to Plymouth, and I was scheduled to work at the community pharmacy the next day. I did not have enough money to book a hotel for the night, and in any case, there was no point.

The next train was at four a.m., a sleeper train for which I had no ticket.

It was looking to be a long, long, night.

I settled on the bench in my dark navy suit that was a little bit too tight for me if I was being honest. It was freezing. Cold.

But I didn't quite feel it.

Because we had just signed to have our own BlueCloud medicines registered in five countries in francophone West Africa.

That's right.

BlueCloud's own branded medicines.

We had pumped over $100,000.00 into registration costs, apart from travel, hotels, and hiring conference rooms in uptown Dubai. And our local partner seemed legit. We had checked him out.

Carry on to July 2021.

The medicines' registration process had been stuck in La La Land for four years. A change in government in Benin and instability in Côte d'Ivoire hadn't helped.

But then we had the phone call—the medicines had been registered. But our local partner suddenly disappeared. He wouldn't pick up my calls, answer my emails, or acknowledge my texts.

Il avait disparu dans les airs, pour ne plus jamais être revu.

And that's how, as his consultant, I had a $100,000.00 lawsuit slapped on my head.

And that's what you call betrayal.

And I still have no idea where he is.

THE PAIN OF PHD

In the 80s and 90s when Africa was going through its dark days, and coup d'états were the order of the day, *The Economist* labelled Africa the hopeless continent.[40]

It stung, not just because of the words, but because of its truth.

Poverty, corruption, extrajudicial killings, a total disregard for human rights, and the effects of the Cold War were rampant.

Dictators ruled as they saw fit, and dog ate dog.

In my native Ghana, we coined the phrase "Pull Him Down," which was a play on the Doctor of Philosophy (PhD) degree.

PhD, which describes what other people will do or say to us to keep us where they think we are supposed to be, not where we know we should be.

The Olympic Games in Tokyo have just ended, and I am always fascinated by the long-distance runs. There are always a few at the back, a huge clog in the middle, and a few out front. In the last 800 meters or so, runners try to break out and make a beeline for the finish line. Only a few make

---

40 The Economist, 13 May 2000

it, and even fewer still to the medal zone. Winning a medal in long-distance races is hard.

And so is breaking out from the comfort of a well-paying, secure job, living with parents, or being an employee. That's where you are likely to meet the PhDs. People who, either for good reasons or bad, resent you trying to leave the fold and breaking out to try to follow your dreams. And not all PhDs are bad.

Michael is the CEO of a healthcare and agricultural consultancy called GSL based in Blantyre, Malawi, and prior to the founding of his company, he worked as a public health specialist consultant with the NHS, in Kent, England.

In 2017 he formed GSL and made the jump to Malawi to pursue his dream of encouraging investment and starting a healthcare chain of clinics, as well as encouraging investment in that poor landlocked country in East Africa. But his close friends and family had other ideas. Especially when things didn't work out as planned, and he lost out on a lucrative power supply contract to the newly elected government at the last minute.

It was a "take it or leave it" thing. Either come back to the UK and continue to live a comfortable life as a public health consultant and be part of the family—or be on your own and follow the dream in your heart.

He tried his best to make both work. His family wouldn't budge, so he had to take the plunge. I could feel the pain in his voice as I spoke to him on the phone. It brought tears to my eyes and reminded me of the comments I received from my professional friends after six years of trial and error with BlueCloud:

"I told you going to study business after your pharmacy degree was a waste of time."

"I think you should do this new course and get paid more money—that's the trend everyone else is following now."

"You should be content with what you have—why do you want to put yourself through all this hassle?"

And it's hard to argue with their logic. Especially when you see the trappings of success they have with the safe path they have followed—the new car, the new house, the holidays, the pictures on social media—whilst you are stuck. Your roots need to be strong to resist and keep going. That's why the Honeymoon Period is so crucial.

THE PAIN OF CARING

I just wanna know oh oh
When did you get so cold oh oh oh
What happened to your soul oh oh oh
I thought that we were close
But now that door is closed
What happened to your soul oh oh oh
When did we lose control?

- NF, "I Just Wanna Know," *Therapy Session*, 2016

Feels like we're on the edge right now
I wish that I could say I'm proud
I'm sorry that I let you down
I let you down
You don't wanna know my hurt, yet
Let me guess...

- NF, "Let You Down," *Perception*, 2020

This is the toughest pain I have had to face. By far.

The pain of loneliness.

It's terrible.

It's what drives you to the stupid decisions. The alcohol. The pornography. The gluttony.

Perhaps most difficult is that you experience it with the people who care for you the most. The people you depend on. Your spouse. Your children. Your childhood friends. Your parents. Your co-workers. What's painful is that they care for you, but don't understand you.

But the pain multiplies exponentially because it sows self-doubt, fear, and paranoia. You start thinking to yourself: "These people know me better than anyone else. So maybe I'm the one deluded here. They must be right."

No, they're not. Or are they?

You decide, but bear in mind that decision comes with a price.

I distinctly remember heeding advice to stop what I was doing with Blue-Cloud. I tried to bury it after repeated failures. At last count as I write this, I've experienced more than 250 rejections. My family and friends could see the toll it was taking on me emotionally, financially, and physically. But:

I got a homesick heart but a long ways left to go
I've been doing my part but I ain't got much to show
So I'm asking you to show me some forgiveness
It's all for you in my pursuit of happiness

I got dreams that keep me up in the dead of night
Telling me I wasn't made for the simple life
There's a light I see, but it's far in the distance
I'm asking you to show me some forgiveness
It's all for you in my pursuit of happiness

I've been working all night
Maybe you could help me to believe
So I'm asking you to show me some forgiveness
It's all for you in my pursuit of happiness.

This song called "Happiness" by Grammy-nominated American rock band NEEDTOBREATHE summarises it beautifully.

The conviction that never lets you alone. I tried to hide my phone calls. Even my integrity began to suffer because I started lying to my friends that I had given up BlueCloud for good. I stopped mentioning it to Dela. Or my brother. But...

I could still hear that knock in my dreams
That's why there's no stopping my dreams
No need to fear, just one thing you need to hear...
That knock....

- Shad, "Knock," *Boarding Pass*, 2014

It's that knock that kept Mrs. Bernice Atubra investing in the Henry School and managing it remotely, praying, believing, persuading, even as her husband's health was deteriorating and her children's frustration was rising.

It's that knock that kept Michael in Malawi, working, pressing, even when his own wife had turned her back on him.

And it's that knock that kept me going when most of my close friends and family were laughing in my face and behind my back and called my dream, my purpose, my life a hobby.

I hope that knock will keep you going. It is a green flag, and the corresponding pain is what I call Green Flag Pain. Despite it all, you keep going because:

All I see is green lights
All I see is green lights
All I spit is real life
Bet you don't know what that's like, (huh?)

I know where I'm going
Let no one distract me
I don't need directions from nobody in the back seat
I don't need these people in my corner tryna check me
Yeah, I walk off the bus a different city than the last week.

All I see is green lights....

- NF, "Green Lights," *Perception,* 2020

But there is one major caveat here.

These friends, family, colleagues are not the enemy. They care about you. They see the emotional toll this takes on you and yours. They are aiming to help, not to hinder.

And just like a president needs a senate, or a leader needs a board of directors, you need these guys. I recently had a chat with my wife. I thought she hated the dream. But no. She hated what the dream had done to my health, our marriage, our finances, and my time with the kids.

The dream had become my focus at the expense of everything else, and in the midst of chasing that dream, I was leaving a trail of destruction in my wake.

Just like I did when I crashed down those stairs three weeks ago.

My eyes full of tears, I had to eat humble pie and make some changes quickly.

I had to go back to WGLL, to true north, and a rediscovery of my priorities.

But in the same vein, she also had to learn that this dream of mine was something that I planned to keep working on, right down to my grave.

We made joint changes and promised to stick to them. Time with the kids. Enough sleep. Clear boundaries between work and family. Good diet. Less stress. Time for the marriage. All the things we know to do, but don't. And she promised to protect my time dedicated to the business and to the writing of this book.

But sadly for my friend Michael, it didn't unfold that way.

That same conversation ended up in divorce. His wife refused to acknowledge the burning desire that kept him up at night. She forced him to make a choice that did not have to be made.

Author and Wharton Professor Adam Grant sums up the solution to this problem:

> *The sweet spot of worrying about other people's opinions is caring enough to learn from them, but not so much that you conform to them. It takes humility to rethink your views in the face of disapproval. It takes integrity to put your personal values above social approval.*[41]

The Oxford English Dictionary defines integrity in two ways:

1. The quality of being honest and having strong moral principles

2. The state of being whole and undivided[42]

Both definitions are crucial if you're going to see yourself through Green Flag Pain.

Honesty. Morality. Not a Jekyll and Hyde. Not a '*Gemini Man.*'[43]

But there is one last Green Flag Pain that is caused by another observer.

---

41 https://www.trendsmap.com/twitter/tweet/1490688969096507400 Twitter (@AdamMGrant)
42 Oxford Dictionary Definition (https://www.oxfordlearnersdictionaries.com/definition/english/integrity)
43 https://en.wikipedia.org/wiki/Gemini_Man_(film)

The one Steven Pressfield terms in his *War of Art* book as the Resistance. It is a real observer, but invisible to everyone else apart from ourselves.

GET OUT OF YOUR HEAD

Start the day against the voices
The ones that tell me that I'm wrong
I hear them now
Screaming their delusions
I close my eyes and they're gone

In my mind I hear the voices
In my mind I have my doubts
Burning fears, these ghosts and apparitions
Only a whisper can drown them out, yeah

If they ain't singing
And they're just talking
Let them keep talking to themselves

'Cause everybody knows
The hardest war to fight
Is the fight to be yourself
When the voices try to turn you into someone else
Someone else

- Switchfoot, "Against the Voices," *The Edge of the Earth*, 2014

"I find myself despondent for weeks on end, a weakness, and obstacle to my effectiveness," Bernice Atubra said to me, on lunch in a swanky restaurant in the hills of Devon some weeks ago.

"I have a large family, but no one to depend on, apart from my wife and children; I feel so lonely, and my loneliness attracts lonely people like me," an entrepreneur, Frank, from Ghana confided in me on a recent phone call.

There it is.

The one pain all entrepreneurs face. Loneliness. But the issue isn't really the loneliness. It's the voices that speak to us when we are alone. And the real loneliness begins when we listen and begin to heed those voices.

The little whispering demon perched on our shoulder.

It is the one thing we share in common. The pain it brings trumps all others. If we don't find ways to combat it, our dreams will end up undermined.

How do you deal with this?

You talk back.

We often say here in England that the definition of insanity is when you answer back to yourself.

If that's the case, then I should be the first one in the asylum, chained and sectioned under the English Mental Health Act.[44]

You have to talk to yourself. Stir yourself. Remind yourself why you deserve a seat at the table.

Remind yourself of your Honeymoon Period.

Those voices are not real. They are what they are—just voices—notes floating in the air.

Remember this.

Otherwise, you most certainly will end up as a statistic. One of the failed 90 percent.

---

44 cases when a person can be detained, also known as sectioned, under the English Mental Health Act (1983) and treated without their agreement. (https://www.legislation.gov.uk/ukpga/1983/20/introduction)

AMBER FLAG PAIN:
THE PAIN OF THE MARKET—WAIT

It ought to be plain
How little you gain
By getting excited
And vexed.

You'll always be late
For the previous train,
And always in time
For the next.

- Piet Hein, "Thoughts on a Station Platform"[45]

- Equity Pharmacy, Accra, Ghana
- DrugStoc, Lagos, Nigeria
- RxAll, Lagos Nigeria
- Altics Biologics, Johannesburg, South Africa
- Hospital, Kigali, Rwanda
- Maternova, Providence, RI, United States

---

45 Taken from Matthew, Cerys (Curated) Tell Me the Truth About Life (London, Michael O'Mara Books, 2019)

- Boitekanelo College, Gaborone, Botswana
- Fertility Clinic, Lagos, Nigeria

What do these companies have in common?

Three things.

1. You've probably never heard of them

2. They are all in the healthcare space in Africa

3. They all, at some point, were BlueCloud incubator companies

During my research into healthcare investment in Africa for my MBA, I noticed a big, gaping hole in funding.

That may not surprise you, as Africa is the riskiest continent to invest in, particularly the healthcare sector, at least when informed by the perception of pot-bellied children with houseflies swirling around the mouths and mothers in tears that we see on our televisions here in the West every day.

But my research, after hundreds of papers, interviews, and reviews of existing literature, revealed a surprising truth.

There was no shortage of funds ready and willing to invest in Africa. Some of the big players—Abraaj (now defunct), LeapFrog, IFHA,(Investment Funds for Health in Africa) the IFC (the private investment arm of the World Bank), and many others—had funds in the tens of millions of dollars ready to deploy.

The problem was a lack of investment opportunities for those funds. And there was a clear pattern, borne out in my research and proven on the ground.

There was an excess of interest in the best opportunities on the continent. These were usually organizations which had EBITDA[46] over $15 million. On the other end of the spectrum, there were active angel funds, charities, and investment hubs that catered to small startups with great ideas that needed a small injection of funds below $1 million.

Of course, these funds were hard to access, Africa being Africa, but they were there, if your country had some measure of stability and peace, and you knew where to look.

But as you can probably now see, there was a glaring gap in the market.

The middle market.

Or the "missing middle," a term popularised by my Israeli friend Idit Miller, CEO and founder of EMRC, an organisation dedicated to increasing investment and market interest in Africa.

So I did all the things we were taught in business school. Spot the market opportunity and prepare to fill it.

In my opinion and zeal, this was a market that was ready and bulging, low-hanging fruit for reasons I described earlier on in this book.

So, after graduating from business school, having seen my research validated by a distinction, armed with savings and kind donations from my brother and friends, we started BlueCloud.

We teamed up with EMRC and launched our first BlueCloud AFIF healthcare conference, sponsored by Pfizer, which aimed to unearth middle-sized healthcare companies that wanted to break into the mainstream and present them to investors. They were judged by an eminent panel led

---

46 EBITDA stands for "earnings before interest, taxes, depreciation and amortization" and is used a measure for a company's overall financial performance.

by seasoned healthcare American investor, Les Funtleyder, author of the bestseller *Healthcare Investing* and a regular pundit on CNBC and CNN with a portfolio worth billions. Les had joined BlueCloud and was head of its New York office.

It was a resounding success. There was a competition to award the first Pfizer/AFIF entrepreneur of the conference, held in Cape Town, which was won by Altics Biologics. The interview is featured on our website.

We would offer them leadership skills, help with management, and assist their transition from mom-and-pop stores to real movers and shakers in the African marketplace to effect real change on the healthcare sector.

We opened offices in London, New York, and Johannesburg.

Everything was ready and raring to go.

But after six years of conferences, travelling around the Middle East, Europe, and Africa, we had not secured a single dollar.

The investment world was not ready for Middle Africa.

Welcome to pain caused by the market or, rather, timing of the market.

Amber Flag Pain.

Licking our wounds, and after a cumulative loss of thousands of pounds, we had to return to the drawing table. What had gone wrong? It turns out that our timing was off. The world had yet to catch up with how fast Africa was moving. And the investment tycoons were not ready.

When collating the information, we identified two running themes that had caused our failure.

- Overlooking the REASON why companies bothered to invest in Africa in the first place
- The idiosyncrasies and unique aspects of the African market

A PAT ON THE BACK

Companies tended to invest in Africa to boost their ESG credentials or to genuinely help move the continent forward, in which case it made sense to invest into startups where the need was greatest and the pat on the back was most visible. The other major reason for investment was simply to make money. But in such a risky environment, the benefits of making money would have to vastly outweigh the considerable pitfalls, which was why investment into guaranteed sectors such as the energy sector or the telecommunications sector made sense.

For the startup sector, the investor or charity knew what had to be done: lots and lots of handholding and little guaranteed reward, apart from the warm, fuzzy feeling of knowing that they had put in their penny's worth to move Africa forward.

For the large sector, little handholding, at least in the later stages, but the knowledge that there was a guaranteed huge pay-out at the end.

The middle sector offered neither.

Lots of due diligence, handholding, training, and no guaranteed pay-out. Most private equity houses were not built or designed for the Middle African market.

And we didn't have the credibility and portfolio for them to entrust us with this responsibility.

So we lost out.

But roll on six years, and the investing landscape was changing. I give an example of a successful fund raise later in the book. This time, we were ready to ride the wave.

Even though the example I'm giving here is specific to us, it can be applied to every business sector in every part of the world.

Every entrepreneur is almost guaranteed to have to go through Amber Flag Pain. Since it revolves around timing and market fit, validation is essential.

That's why the poem above by Piet Hein is so relevant a century later and why you should make sure you're ready and waiting for your moment, your shot, as rapper Eminem spells out so well in his famous "Lose Yourself" song.

Amber Flag Pain is not a full stop—it's just a comma. Though it may not be so straightforward for your business, much of the time, the actual pain revolves around waiting.

The antidote is:

W-A-I-T.

We'll talk more about this under the section on the payoff.

Waiting to hear the results of that pitch.

Waiting for that client to pay you the money you're owed.

Waiting for that publisher to land you the book deal.

Waiting, waiting, waiting.

USING THE PAIN RESPONSE MODEL

The pain response model's individual components must not be taken as independent. They are often interlinked, and one can act as a trigger for another. It is crucial to reflect on the generalised pain that we feel as entrepreneurs, leaders, and CEOs. The more regularly and earlier we do this, the better our outcomes will be. We will explore this further in the book under payoff.

For instance, a curt remark from an associate, a friend, or a loved one (Green Flag Pain) may act as a trigger for a self-destructing abusive habit (Red Flag Pain). Once we start to willingly or inadvertently participate in the phantom crutch of Red Flag Pain, deadlines and timelines get missed, shoddier work gets done, and we become a lesser person, which ultimately affects our competition in the market (Amber Flag Pain). If unchecked, this can trigger an illness which causes us to go on a downward spiral (White Flag Pain) which leads to more criticism, curt remarks, etc (Green Flag Pain). And so the cycle continues until it culminates in self-destruction or much-needed change.

So in trying to decipher that curt remark that started it all, you need to drill down to who you are—your identity—which will give you the ability to extract the kernel of truth and let the abusive bits go.

Instead of collapsing or reacting, perhaps you decide to go for a run, listen to your favourite music, or spend time in reflection and prayer, whatever it is that can draw you away from sinking into Red Flag Pain.

Remember, this model does not seek to explain the pain, or give reasons—there are plenty of books, resources, and qualified personnel that can do that better than I could ever dream—but focuses on the **response.**

We can't place ourselves in a bunker, dress ourselves in psychological PPE, and insulate ourselves from the unfair world around us.

But we can certainly give ourselves regular opportunities to reflect on the source of our pain **beforehand** and plan appropriate responses.

This is the stuff of resilience, which we explore in detail further on in the book. But pain, no matter which form it takes, is harder alone. As human beings we are, and always will be, social creatures. You need a confidant, a fellow trooper, a cofounder, a partner because teamwork beats talent. And it's to this crucial element of entrepreneurship that we turn to next.

KEY CONCEPTS:
- Pain response model:
  - Red Flag Pain, the pain of self-sabotage—HALT
  - White Flag Pain, the pain of the unfairness of life—SURRENDER
  - Green Flag Pain, the pain of the observer—GO
  - Amber Flag Pain, the pain of the market—WAIT

QUESTIONS:
1. What is your relationship to pain?

2. Are there types of pain from the model that you recognize from your own life? How did you respond to them when they arose?

3. Are there any that you are battling with right now? How is it affecting your progress as an entrepreneur? How are you planning to get help to get past that hurdle?

THE PARTNER

Brother let me be your shelter
Never leave you all alone
I can be the one you call
When you're low
Brother let me be your fortress
When the night winds are driving on
Be the one to light the way
Bring you home
And when you call
And need me near
Saying where'd you go?
Brother, I'm right here
And on those days
When the sky begins to fall
You're the blood of my blood
We can get through it all

- NEEDTOBREATHE, "Brother," *Rivers in the Wasteland*, 2014

15 August, 2015.

After a whole lot of drama, I landed in Luanda, Angola full of anticipation.

I had just finished organising a very successful healthcare conference for investors in Cape Town, South Africa, cosponsored by the pharmaceutical giant Pfizer, and flown to Gabarone, Botswana to sign a deal for a multi-million diagnostics centre.

On the flight from Gaborone to Johannesburg, there was an old woman I sat close to who struggled to carry her luggage from the plane. So I stopped to help her—she could hardly walk.

That good deed had bad consequences, but looking at the pain in her eyes as she struggled to walk, it was all worth it.

As I helped her to get her luggage to her next connecting flight, I saw out of the corner of my eye that the flight from Johannesburg to Luanda was boarding.

I practically ran to the checkout point, and the plane had finished boarding, and I could see the gate was closed.

I was desperate to get on that plane.

There was a $16 million state-of-the-art diagnostic centre and a $5 million wholesale medicines deal on the line. I needed to get onto that flight.

The traffic crew refused to let me board that plane.

I dropped to my knees and practically begged them.

I could see the plane beginning to taxi. I was beside myself. I was almost in tears. Actually, I was in tears.

The supervisor could see the desperation in my pleading.

Finally, the ground crew radioed the pilot, who agreed to stop.

To cut a long story short, I finally got onto that plane. I could feel the eyes of the passengers and crew tunnelling into my flesh as I sheepishly crawled into my seat.

Two hours later, I was in Luanda, then the world's most expensive city.

But in the melee, and to add insult to injury (or due to some kind of error), my luggage had been lost. Everything was gone, and I had nothing left apart from my wallet and my hand luggage.

Absolutely nothing. Or, as they say in Portuguese, nada.

I had landed in the most expensive city in the world at that time with nothing but my wallet and a small bag. I didn't speak the language, I had no friends or acquaintances there, and I was at the total mercy of my Angolan and Portuguese hosts.

To sign my first-ever multimillion deal.

So, a shopping spree had to go onto my Barclays credit card. Food, new clothes, toiletries, hotel bill at $250 per night for an apology of a hotel. There was a reason Luanda at that time was the world's most expensive city.

The credit card bill at the end of the month was not pretty.

I hid the bill from my wife, buried the card in the deepest recesses of my wallet, and pushed the memory of that bill to the trash bin of my mind.

I was here to save the world.

BlueCloud was three years old, and I was fresh out of business school. My passion was high, my hopes were rocketing, and the stars shone out my eyes.

I was slated to meet with the CEO of a multimillion-dollar company with interests in real estate, oil and gas, and hospitality.

The contrast between the poverty I saw in Luanda and the opulence of our local partner was staggering.

I was there to validate our local partner to make sure he was who he said he was.

He had land, cars, everything. And he appeared honest.

I had a fresh new suit, swanky shoes, and expensive perfume, all purchased the day before in Luanda's brand-new shopping centre on a hidden credit card. I looked the part, externally at least.

Two years later, after multiple meetings in Nairobi, Lagos, and again in Luanda, the deal was signed.

BlueCloud was set to make its first million dollars, together with its sister company in Delhi, only a year after we had graduated from business school and formed the company.

Then all hell broke loose.

The government of Angola was done in—the famous dos Santos family had fled the country, and a new era was born.

The deal, which had been signed, was shelved. The new government was not interested.

And that was that.

15 July, 2021.

Roll forward five years. Our investing partners had apparently lost interest. My calls, emails, and WhatsApp messages were unanswered.

No activity whatsoever.

We spent the intervening years building up the business. We opened an office and registered the business in Dubai, opened another office in London, and employed staff to do the normal expansion stuff. Costs ran into the tens of thousands of dollars. We named the parent company Emerald, which would be headquartered in a plush office complex in the heart of Dubai, UAE.

It was a 'build it and they will come' phase.

Then things begin to happen. Rumours and whispers, difficult to verify.

The third partners had gone behind our backs and were doing big business with another local partner. We had no idea. There had been no official confirmation.

When I say big business, I mean big business.

Hundreds of millions of dollars' worth of business were changing hands. Medicines, expertise, trade, cosmetics.

In the murky world of Africa, this was all possible.

We and our local partners had been completely cut out of the deal, due in large part to our inexperience and naiveté. To be honest, we had also pushed a bit too hard when things were not going well and rubbed a few shoulders the wrong way.

We lost out, big time.

This sent me into a deep depression and burnout, exacerbated my health issues, and nearly ruined my career. I am still feeling the effects today.

Simply speaking, our bulls*t detection—reading people's intentions and having a sense of where their incentives lie—was lacking at the time, and as Ash Ali and Hasan Kubba pointed out in their 2021 U.K. Business Book of the Year *The Unfair Advantage*: people skills can often be more important than having an MBA from a top business school or being incredibly intelligent.[47]

Nevertheless, that did not excuse the way we had been treated.

---

47 Ali & Kubba, The Unfair Advantage, (London Profile Books, 2020)

The costs had become too much for BlueCloud. The credit card bills had mounted.

The final straw came when I did not have enough money to pay for my wife's birthday meal, and she had to pay for a meal I had organised.

A month or so later, we went shopping at a supermarket that dealt with nearly expired groceries. That's how bad things had become.

The bill came to only £20.

I could not afford to pay.

Things came to a head.

I made the long-delayed call to the bankruptcy company the next morning and went on a debt repayment plan. I narrowly averted complete bankruptcy.

I was broke, financially and emotionally.

And not long after, in a matter of months, I lost my father-in-law and sister, and the epilepsy that had lain dormant for so long came raging back.

Things were bad, very bad, and I had a hit a new low.

The time had come to throw in the towel, but that feeling, that tug, that hay that I had built in the Honeymoon Period, was still burning deep within me.

I couldn't let everything go—I just couldn't.

Luckily, I had my pharmacy occupation to fall back on. That kept the lights on and the bills paid.

It was at that time that I learnt the biggest business lesson of my life.

Paper up!

This is what entrepreneur, lecturer, and environmental policy consultant Dr. Abena Asomaning Antwi, author of the book *Purposeful Chaos,* says:

IT'S NECESSARY TO PAPER UP!
Often people get into agreements with other parties, particularly people they consider friends and family, without any formal documentation. Let me let you in on a few hard truths:

1. People seem desperate and honest when they require professional services
2. Human beings tell lies. Plain and simple
3. People develop amnesia once the job is done
4. Money changes people's attitudes
5. It's only business, no hard feelings

Between 2019-2020, I rendered consultancy services for people I considered true and honest friends. I trusted their word of timely payment upon completion of work. I put in the time, tirelessly. They weren't going anywhere, they said, whenever I talked about a contract. They were very happy with my services until the point when they needed to pay me. Then they suddenly stopped responding to emails, calls, and text messages. Wow. Who could I blame for this? Even though they chose the path of deceit, should I have bothered to take a legal route? I decided against it. But I bagged lessons for future interactions. Friendship, business and lies don't mix. So PAPER UP! Document the business agreements by all means, friend or not. You are not "too officious" if they complain of mistrust. Trusting everyone is just too pricey.[48]

Wise words.

Partnerships can make or break your business. It's important that you get them right.

But how?

---

48 Asomaning, Abena Dr. – Quote from LinkedIn Post. Used with permission.

BONDING IN PARTNERSHIPS

In today's hyper-connected world, partnerships, and collaborations have become an indispensable part of business. In relatively small consultancies like Emerald or BlueCloud, which have localised small teams but a global ambition and reach, this is a reality that cannot be avoided. In fact, partnerships, networking, and connections are things that we actively encourage, not only because they extend our reach across the world, but also because they allow us to engage with people who have real local knowledge, who are experts in their fields, and who can save us tons of energy, money, time, and a truckload of mistakes.

It's unfortunate that when we started Emerald, we understood this from the start, but we didn't introduce the frameworks or models to carefully choose the kinds of partners we could work with or a method by which to choose them.

Generally speaking, we knew that they should be trustworthy, ethical, have a good experience portfolio in the country or field in which they worked, and should be team players.

But, as we soon found out, this was nowhere near enough.

This basic model was found wanting, especially in the parts of the world where we had decided to ply our trade: Africa, Asia, and the Middle East.

So, as the Russian cliché goes: **Doveryai, No Proveryai**

This Russian proverb, which literally means "A responsible person always certifies," points to the need to check and verify everything before committing to business with anyone, even if that anyone is totally trustworthy.

Its popularity in the West is anecdotally ascribed to President Ronald Reagan.

The greatest mistake we can make in partnerships as ethical entrepreneurs is assuming that everyone makes a business deal for symbiotic purposes.

This cannot be further from the truth.

This is not to say, as I will explain further on in this section, that most people are criminals, liars, or thieves and deserve to go to prison.

Of course not.

I still believe in the basic goodness of humanity and that the vast majority of people really do mean to do what they set out to do.

But integrity and character extend far beyond that.

They involve the realization that a good partnership only succeeds if both partners actively look out for the success of the deal, which means not just for themselves, but also for one another.

The key word here is **actively.**

These partnerships must be actively monitored, verified, and continually reviewed in the light of new information.

In monitoring these partnerships, a few questions need to be asked:

- How long do I intend this partnership to last?
- What are the characteristics I am willing to be flexible about?
- How closely knit is this partnership likely to be?
- And how can I look out for the best interests (and vice versa) of this person/business I am getting myself into?

In his revolutionary bestseller, *Give and Take*, author Adam Grant demonstrates how giving more to others, rather than just competing against them, may be the greatest secret to real success and leaving a good legacy.

So, start with who.

We need to be givers in a partnership. Driven by the desire to help others, create lasting success for the group, and focus on the greater good.

Even though we may go into a partnership with this attitude, the extent to which we can give or take is shaped by who we interact with.

Looking back at the hundreds of deals we lost, failed to get over the line, or got over the line only to end up being manipulated later, we realised that we had to get things in place to avoid falling again into the same traps.

But how is this done in practice?

As I thought about this while writing the book, I realized there was already a workable model, but it wasn't in business. It was formulated 158 years ago by a then-little-known Russian scientist who happened to be killing time on a train. Dmitri Mendeleev.

On that train on 17 February, 1869, he invented the Periodic Table, which the *New Scientist* called "perhaps the greatest breakthrough in the history of chemistry." But here, I have expanded this theory to be used as a kind of model for understanding partnerships and other relationships in business. The kinds of bonds—ionic, covalent and polar covalent—and the types of elements—broadly metallic and non-metallic—can be used to understand how to form partnerships in business.

In 1869, Dmitri Medeleev published a paper entitled, "On the Relationship of the Properties of the Elements to Their Atomic Weights," where he listed the elements in order of increasing weight and arranged them in groups based on similar chemical properties. It took decades for his principle to be accepted, but it's now become the bedrock of chemistry and formed the basis for the periodic table of the elements.

Even though further developments in science have refined Mendeleev's original table, the principle remains intact: "The arrangement according to atomic weight corresponds to the valence of an element, and, to a certain extent, the difference in chemical behaviour."[49]

About 50 years after this paper, scientists discovered that the atom is built around a nucleus with positively charged protons and neutral neutrons, which is surrounded by a cloud of negatively charged electrons.

The electrons in the cloud surrounding an element's nucleus are arranged in layers, called shells.

Each shell has a s specific number of electrons it can hold.

When the shell is filled, another shell is added until all of the electrons are accounted for.

Electrons in the outermost shell are called valence electrons because their interactions with electrons of other elements determine the element's chemical properties and behaviour.

Though it may be something of a simplification, all elements in the periodic table can be spoken of as metals and non-metals.

Metals make up the left side of the periodic table and non-metals the right side.

Compounds are formed by the interaction of elements through a process called chemical bonding and are predicted by a concept called electronegativity.

Electronegativity is a measure of an atom's ability to attract shared electrons to itself. On the periodic table, electronegativity generally increases as you move from left to right across a period and decreases as you move down

---

49 https://sciencing.com/elements-valence-electrons-relate-its-group-periodic-table-23326.html

a group. As a result, most electronegative elements are found on the top right of the periodic table, and the most electropositive are found in the bottom left. The more electronegativity elements have, the more likely they are to form ionic bonds.

The goal of all chemical bonding is to reach the most stable (lowest energy) state possible. Many atoms become stable when their valence shell is filled with electrons. If atoms don't have this arrangement, they strive to reach it by gaining, losing, or sharing electrons via bonds.

Ionic bonds tend to be stronger and more stable, and the resultant compounds are formed from the transfer of electrons from one element to the other.

They are typically formed from elements on the far-left side of the periodic table (metals which tend to have excess number of valence electrons in their outermost shell) and elements on the right side of the table (non-metals, which tend to have a lesser number of valence electrons in their outermost shell).

Elements with electrons to spare (positively charged) bond with elements that lack electrons (negatively charged). An example is the combination of sodium and chloride, which makes sodium chloride, or table salt.

However, ionic bonds can easily be broken if they are in the right environment. Salt also exemplifies this feature of ionic bonds. Its crystal bonds are extremely stable in a vacuum but are instantly broken when dissolved in water. This paradox also plays out in business partnerships.

Covalent bonds tend to be weaker than ionic bonds and are formed when elements come together to share electrons, rather than fully gaining or losing them. They typically are formed by non-metallic elements (so they are similar and crowded around the same area of the periodic table) and are more common. For example, they make up the structure of carbon-based organic molecules like DNA and proteins, as well as that of smaller inorganic molecules like water, (H_2O), carbon dioxide, (CO_2) and oxygen

(O_2). One, two, or three pairs of electrons may be shared between atoms, resulting in **single, double, or triple** bonds. The more electrons shared, the stronger the bond will be.

There are two kinds of covalent bonds, polar and non-polar covalent bonds, and again, this can largely be predicted by Mendeleev's periodic table. The Khan Academy explains this concept in more detail[50]:

> In **polar covalent bonds,** electrons are unequally shared by the atoms and spend more time in proximity to one atom due to the differences in electronegativity. For instance, in water, oxygen is more electronegative than hydrogen, which means that it attracts the shared electrons more strongly. As a result, the oxygen in water bears a partial negative charge (has more electrons) than hydrogen. So polar covalent bonds exhibit some characteristics of an ionic bond and some of a covalent bond.

In **non-polar covalent bonds**, the electrons are shared between two atoms of the same element or between different elements more or less equally. The Khan Academy online tutorial uses methane (CH_4) as an example:

> Carbon has four electrons in its outermost shell and needs four more to achieve a stable octet. It gets these by sharing electrons with four hydrogen atoms, each of which provides a single electron. Reciprocally, the hydrogen atoms each need one additional electron to fill their outermost shell, which they receive in the form of shared electrons from carbon.

> Although carbon and hydrogen do not have exactly the same electronegativity, they are quite similar, so carbon hydrogen bonds are considered non-polar.

So the obvious question: how is this applicable to the real business world?

I realised that all of the partners we'd worked with over the preceding decade fell into three categories:

---

50 Khan Academy, The Periodic Table (https://www.khanacademy.org/science/chemistry/periodic-table)

- The partner or cofounder(s)
- The partners
- The collaborators

And in following in the general theme of this book, there seemed to be two kinds of partnerships, very generally speaking, depending on which part of the world we were working in, the timescales involved, and the goal of the partnership:

- relational partnerships
- transactional partnerships

The model below simplifies my thinking behind how to work with partners:

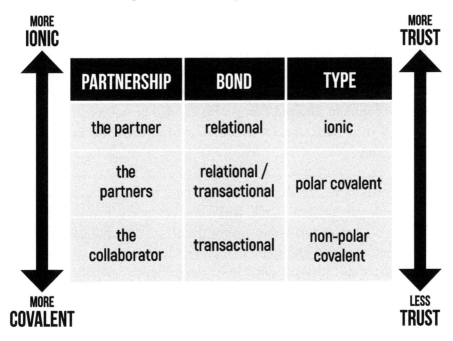

THE COFOUNDER PARTNER
OR THE IONIC BOND

The strongest bond that can be formed in business is probably with your cofounder or long-term partner.

Abhinav Srivastava is an incredible individual.

How we became friends and partners is still unclear—all I remember is an email and a message on LinkedIn about a potential way we could collaborate on deals in Africa. He reached out to me just after he'd finished business school and I was in my final year at Warwick. He had just founded his strategic consulting firm, The Strategy Boutique (it had to have *the* in the name, so he keeps reminding me) and started to consult for some pretty large companies in Asia and Europe. He decided he wanted to extend the reach of TSB to Africa, so, for reasons that still remain unclear to me, he contacted me.

On the surface, we are incredibly dissimilar. He was born and raised in India, is 15 years my junior, tall, lanky, and extremely fit with a receding hairline. He has an incredible eye for detail, is very opinionated, has a strong character and knows how to party. He is a typical citizen of the world—born in India; educated in England; holidays regularly in Latin America; spends a large amount of his time in the Middle East; has business interests in France, Columbia, and Africa; and does not share my optimism and passion for Africa or my eclectic taste in music or poetry.

We are in completely different professions. Abhinav trained as an economist; I am a qualified pharmacist. My entire training has been in pharmacy and health; his has been in management and consultancy.

But under the bonnet, we are incredibly similar. We share our "non-negotiable," fierce commitment to ethical principles, are incredibly resilient, and believe firmly in people and collaboration, but cling to ideals of independence. We are both fiercely protective of our business sources, are not very good at the 'boring stuff,' and are dogged to the point of stupidity, sometimes.

The motto for The Strategy Boutique is "Honest Consulting," to give you an idea of the sort of person he is.

Our partnership has lasted for nearly 10 years and shows no signs of slowing. We've lost tens of thousands of pounds together, have failed at hundreds of deals, and have had bitter disagreements and quarrels—one culminating in in the near-dissolution of the partnership.

We never knew our partnership would still be going strong after that first call in 2014, but looking back, it has stood the test of time and contributed immensely to this part of the book.

The bond between you and the partner should be an ionic bond.

To trust unconditionally means to be careless. Not careless in the sense of being disorganised, but there is a much greater degree of trust here. It is the kind of trust that rests on a mutual, dynamic regard for one another's interests. This goes beyond a symbiotic partnership—it means each of us will actively look out for what is good for both of us.

Dr. Harry Cloud puts it this way:

> You do not have to 'watch your back' with him, because he is going to be watching it for you. So if something comes up in the deal later that neither of you thought of, you know that the person on the other side of the table is going to be concerned

for your interests as well as his own. He won't be a pushover, but he will have concern for you too, even when he doesn't have to.[51]

This is what it means to be "careless."

It means that we don't have to worry about how to take care of ourselves with one another, because we are looking out for one another and concerned about each other, even when he doesn't have to.

Deciding on a partner and cofounder is possibly the most crucial decision you can make in your business. A Steven Wozniak to Steve Jobs, or a Larry Page and Sergey Brin to Google, or Adam Lowry and Eric Ryan in Method—or, to extend beyond business, Barack Obama and Joe Biden. One is everything the other is not. The bond is an attractive trust, and it's for the long haul.

An ionic bond.

As humans, we are made to work best in partnerships, and it's possible that the single greatest mistake in starting a substantial business undertaking we make is thinking we could be the single founder or sole trader.

In finding a partner or in cofounding, there must be three elements:

- The 'non-negotiables'
- The demands of reality
- The dominance of the relational partnership

Non-negotiables:

If you're reading this book, then your non-negotiables should be clear. If you sign up to be an ethical entrepreneur, then there is no room for

---

51 Cloud, Henry: Integrity: The Courage to Meet the Demands of Reality (New York, Harper Business, 2009) Page 77f

manoeuvring—you stand by the principles enumerated earlier in the Honeymoon Period.

In fact, the fiercest arguments and disagreements Abhinav and I have had in business revolve around those principles and whether they have been compromised by either of us. They are principles that stand the test and rigours of time and tide, irrespective of the sector, field, location, or type of deal we have worked on. This is another reason your Honeymoon Period should be firm and immovable.

The Demands of Reality:

Let me never fall into the vulgar mistake of dreaming that I am persecuted whenever I am contradicted.

- Ralph Waldo Emerson

In choosing a long-term partner, you should be able to take a long and good hard look at the real you. As I write this, I am sitting in a room next to where I fell down the stairs, and I can see from the door the destruction I left.

I spoke earlier about the principle of the trail for an ethical entrepreneur.

You need to look at your strengths and weaknesses without any self-pity and know where you need help. And help can come by way of working on ourselves or by way of partnerships.

I am a big-picture type of guy, and I can see the overall vision of where I want to be. I tend to be very creative and a deep thinker, and I can solve problems by thinking out of the box. But the downside of this is my tendency to overlook the details. I'm not good with operations, procedures, and in-the-box stuff, and I tend to procrastinate. I find budgeting hard and have to work at being orderly and organised. I tend to be easy-going and laid-back. I am good with relationships, but not so good with tasks.

So I need to have the self-awareness to know what I lack and look for those strengths in my partners.

Abhinav is my opposite. He's on time, good with procedures, disciplined, and extremely professional. So we complement each other very well, and that's why the partnership works.

There is something interesting I have noticed after working with him for ten years. My 'trail' is getting better. I am getting better with tasks, and I'd like to think he is getting better with relationships. Working with him has improved my character.

That's what the right partner does. You get better by working with him, and results get better because whether we like it or not, we will be judged by our results.

Results matter. They are the wake from which we get evaluated, judged, and 'for which we strive to bring our dreams into reality.'

The Dominance of the Relational Partnership:

I compare the bond between the partner with the ionic bond I described earlier. The bond between the partner goes beyond NDAs, MOUs, and contracts. It is built on trust, truth, and connection, just as the ionic bond between metals and non-metals is based on giving and taking. I need what you have, and I have what you need.

With that said, making it work is hard work.

So what is a relational partnership?

It is a partnership based on relationship—on the premise of a close, trusting relationship where there is an open line of communication and parties work together constantly to resolve any differences. But

the hallmark of this kind of partnership is that even if you fail to reach a goal, the partnership remains. You're in for the long haul.

Ionic bonds can also easily be broken in the wrong environment. I gave the example of sodium chloride being dissolved in water, though it is virtually unbreakable in a vacuum. A partnership of this kind thrives in a solid atmosphere of trust, integrity, and shared ethical principles. Remove these and the bond dissolves, just like salt in water.

In my childhood home in Accra, Ghana, I lived near Ghana's biggest salt factory.

Every morning, I used to watch as the labourers dug the salt from the salt ponds and stacked them for bagging and transport. In the dry weather (called harmattan), those salt crystals could be stacked for months without any damage. However, come the rain, they performed a disappearing act. Here today, gone tomorrow. The strength and the weakness of an ionic bond.

THE TRANSACTIONAL PARTNER
OR THE POLAR COVALENT BOND

When I started BlueCloud, I had the dream to reach every corner of sub-Saharan Africa with healthcare investments, quality medicines, and good management training. I didn't have the resources or time to travel through every country, so I proceeded to find like-minded people who were in the same field as I was and lived in the countries I wanted to reach.

In other words, I needed partners.

I got this model of working from the sales guru, Anderson Hirst, CEO and founder of Selling Interactions, one of the foremost selling consultancies in the country, whom I quoted earlier in this book. Anderson has achieved international success with global companies through his work with partners. It's the only way such a small firm could achieve wide-reaching continental success.

You may never have heard of Selling Interactions, but you will have heard of his clients: Warwick Business School, Volvo Trucks, Aspire Sports, Cushman and Wakefield, and many others.

His sales excellence diagnostic tool has been used with success in over 14 countries throughout Europe. When forming Selling Interactions, he invested time and energy in finding like-minded independent sales executives throughout Europe—some of them are listed on the company website.

Finding partners has peculiar similarities with the polar covalent bond I have described earlier. The attraction comes from shared interests—being in the same field—but also shared values. Anderson talks a lot about trust, character, reliability, and integrity, the non-negotiables.

Selling Interactions has been able to reach markets worldwide including mainland Europe, Japan, and the United States by working with sales professionals who have a similar background, but also share relational aspects.

In other words, part of the strength of the bond comes from shared interests, but also from attractions to the same ideals—a blend of relational and transactional partnerships.

To give a practical example:

Dr. Dayo Sobamowo is a qualified medical doctor and the head of Hermes Consulting in Lagos, Nigeria.

He has decades of experience in healthcare consulting in Nigeria, having worked with international companies such as Zipline, the World Bank, and Shell.

He and I are Africans of a similar age, are passionate about Africa, and are educated in the UK with MBAs with a specialization in market entry.

He knows the Nigerian healthcare market far more than I do, so it makes sense for BlueCloud to work with Hermes on all our deals involving Nigeria. He has the local expertise; BlueCloud has the market entry resources needed.

We have an MOU in place which involves everything from sharing revenue to SOPs on how we work together.

But over the years, we've also built an understanding of trust, integrity, and friendship.

So why did I search out Dayo? The primary reason was to find someone local I could work with when doing deals in Nigeria. While this was a shared goal, there also needed to be the attraction of working together since we planned to collaborate on multiple deals. But these multiple deals were limited to one geographical location: Nigeria.

To return to an earlier point, you want to paper up with this kind of partnership. However, the strength of the bond also depends on the strength of something you can't sign on the dotted line, namely a good, open relationship.

In addition to what I've already said, there is a unique feature of the polar covalent bond: the power balance. Electrons are shared unequally in a polar covalent bond.

The atom that has the strongest electronegativity tends to pull the shared electrons closest to itself. The larger the difference, the more ionic the bond tends to be.

This has implications for business partnerships in two ways:

- **Know who has the power in the partnership**: Most partnerships are not equal. A small farmer entering into a partnership with a large supermarket to supply potatoes. A small supplier of microchips entering into a partnership with Apple. Clearly, as in a polar covalent bond, power is shared unequally. You need to assess, evaluate, accept, and work with the power discrepancies to form a successful partnership.
- **Just like polar covalent bonds, most partnerships in business are a mixture of Eastern relational partnerships (ionic bonds) and Western transactional partnerships (covalent bonds)**: In her brilliant book *The Culture Map: Breaking through the Invisible Boundaries of Global Business*, Erin Meyer groups cultures as high-task-based to high-relationship-based.

High-relationship-based countries tend to be Eastern (but also include other countries such as Brazil) and form their relationships based on shared personal experiences. In China, for instance, an agreement cannot be reached until they have developed what is known as guanxi. So time, effort, and energy must be expended to establish an emotional connection with people from such cultures.

However, in high-task-based cultures such as the UK, US, and the Netherlands, partnerships are created by means of business-related achievements. Depending on how good it is for business or profits, a relationship can be forged or dissolved easily. It's the contract between both parties that counts, not the relationship. Difficulties are likely to be solved in the courtroom, not at the dinner table.

THE COLLABORATOR PARTNER
OR THE NON-POLAR COVALENT BOND

I gave the example of the story of the problems we had in Angola to show the dangers of working with collaborators.

Now, the people we worked with on the Angola deal (which, by the way, is now worth hundreds of millions of dollars) are not bad people. They are not criminals. They will not lie, cheat, or steal and are competent at their jobs.

But in working with collaborators, remember that the shared interests boil down to one thing: the deal.

Nothing more; nothing less. Once the deal is done, the relationship is done. Purely transactional.

It's that terrifyingly simple.

I recently reread an excerpt from the book *Integrity* by Dr. Henry Cloud, whom I quoted earlier, and it sums up beautifully what working with collaborators is all about:

A friend came up to Dr. Henry Cloud and asked him about how to work with a mutual client (called 'Joe') and whether he would recommend him.

This was his answer:

> "I am fumbling a little bit here to get this right. I really like Joe, and he is enormously talented. He is honest, and will not lie, cheat, or steal. He will basically do what he tells you he will do. So all of that is good, and you can trust it."

"So what are you stumbling over or not saying?" my friend asked.

"Well, here is the only way I know how to say it. Make sure that in writing you absolutely, 100 percent protect your interests and get contracts and commitments for everything you are going to need. Make sure that everything that is important to you is protected, in writing."

"That sounds awfully like he is not trustworthy. If he is so honest and has integrity, why would I have to worry so much about watching out for my interests?" my friend asked, somewhat confused.

I understood his confusion, as it is the kind of confusion that people feel when there is a basically good person in their life that they would not, for some reason, trust with the deepest aspects of their heart. How could I explain it?

"Here is the best way to say it: you have to worry about your interests, **because he is not going to**," I said. "He will not lie to you or steal from you, and he will do what he says he is going to do. But he is only going to be thinking about what is good for him, not what is good for you. He is not going to be looking out for your interests, so **make sure you do** (emphasis mine). That is what I mean."

"I still don't quite understand," my friend said.

"I would have ironclad contracts with really smart lawyers, so he will have to do what you need and not do what you don't want. If you do that, and negotiate those things upfront, then you will be happy."

My friend went ahead and did the deal.

It worked out well for him and was successful.

About three years later, I ran into him at a party, and he walked up to me and said, "Thank you for your advice. I did exactly what you told me to do, and it has worked out well. But I did 100 percent see what you were talking about, and if I had not tied up everything up very tight, I would not like where I would be now.

"He does what he agrees to but is not really looking out for anybody else in the process. There are things he would not have done if I had not tied him up contractually. So if I had not done that, I don't think it would be so good."

"Glad it worked out," I said. "Would you do it again?"

He just looked at me.

I knew what he meant.[52]

When I read this, I nearly cursed under my breath.

I wished I had read this just three years earlier.

Deals in my career have been littered with failed transactions like this. Especially in Africa, where my assumptions of shared culture and values had been utterly shattered, because I thought crossing the t's and dotting the i's were not as important as cultivating the relationship.

So that is the covalent bond in partnership. The bond is transactional.

And depending on the deal, and the collaborators you're working with, everything, **even the non-negotiables,** must be tied up in a contract.

Basically, the less you trust, the stronger the covalent (contractual) bonds should be.

In covalent bonding, you have single, double, or even triple bonds.

So remember, the less the trust, the stronger the bond(s) has to be.

Simple.

---

52 Cloud, Henry: Integrity: The Courage to meet the demands of reality (New York, Harper Business, 2009)

But as Anderson states, regardless of whether partnerships are transactional or relational, being a good human being is crucial to get past disagreements and solve even the most difficult issues that arise as an inherent risk in forming partnerships.

So again, this dials down again to the five principles of being an ethical entrepreneur.

There's no getting away from that.

But choosing a partner is one thing that is within your control. But unfortunately, like tossing a coin, somethings you don't get to control.

As Grammy-award-winning band Switchfoot say in their song "Vice Verses," *Every blessing comes with a set of curses, I got my vices, I got my vice verses.*

Or, as Newton Third's Law says, every reaction has an opposite and equal reaction. And it's this dynamic of choices and their reactive consequences in business that we turn to next.

The payoff.

KEY CONCEPTS:
- Paper Up!
- Bonding in Partnerships using Mendeleev's Concept of the Periodic Table:
  - The Partner or the Ionic Bond
  - The Partners or the Polar Covalent Bond
  - The Collaborators or the Non-polar Covalent Bond

QUESTIONS
1. Where are you in the process of forming partnerships?
2. Are there particular partnerships that stand in your business circle that need restructuring after reading this chapter? If so, what are they and why?

THE PAYOFF

"You can't be that good and work so hard at what you do for such a long time and it not pay off in the end. The giant looks in the mirror and sees nothing.**"**

Donda West

You got your babies
I got my hearses
Every blessing comes with a set of curses
I got my vices
Got my vice verses...

- Switchfoot, "Vice Verses," *Vice Verses*, 2011

10 September, 2021.

Emma Raducanu has made history as the youngest British tennis player to win the US Open final and the first British woman since Virginia Wade (53 years ago) to do so.

To win the competition, she beat Maria Sakari of Greece in straight sets in the semi-final. The 18-year-old from Bromley is ranked 150th in the world, and this is her only second Grand Slam.

Sky News called her an "overnight sensation."

But really, the signs had been coming.

She was ranked 338th at the last Wimbledon championships, and she beat three of the world's best players to get to the last 16, where she had to pull out due to breathing difficulties.

Understandably, she was gutted.

But her now-famed resilience and determination showed—she got her A-level results, an A star in maths and an A in economics, just five days later after her dramatic exit at Wimbledon.

Accomplished celebrities, such as Liam Gallagher and Gary Lineker, began to recognise her talent and led the country to gather behind her, and footballer Marcus Rashford led commiserations when she had to give up.

One of the best possible decisions she made was not to look at social media during the tournament—she handed her phone to her physical therapist for safekeeping, which probably meant she avoided the comments by controversial broadcasters Piers Morgan and John McEnroe suggesting she gave up because she didn't have the mental fortitude for the sport.

She also chose not to hold offences against anyone. "There is always going to be someone who has something to say, and I respect everyone's thoughts and decisions, **so I don't really hold anything against anyone**," she says, in her interview with *Vogue* magazine in September 2021 (emphasis mine). [53]

But was she really an overnight sensation?

Despite being a full-time student, she had a backbreaking schedule, day, after day. She had three to four hours on the court, followed by extra time in the gym. She worked on her schoolwork in between sessions.

She'd always been an outdoor girl who loved sport. But which one?

Her dad, being Romanian, and her Chinese mom started her off with motorsports, tap lessons, golf, dirt bike racing, ballet, and then tennis. But as time went on, the others fell by the wayside, through what she calls 'natural selection,' though she still remains passionate about motorcycle

---

53 https://www.vogue.co.uk/arts-and-lifestyle/article/emma-raducanu-interview

racing. But that has taken a backseat. She credits her focus, hardworking ethic, and inner strength to her parents.

In an interview with *Vogue* Magazine (who also used the phrase "appeared out of nowhere") in September 2021:

> But her parents remain the people Raducanu wants to impress the most—and who, perhaps, remain the hardest to. "They're very tough to please and have high expectations," she says. "So that's a big driving factor as to why I want to perform." They're not ones given to big celebrations. Instead, their role has been "to keep me grounded," she continues. "I think they've done a really great job. Because I don't feel like anything is different, in a way. I was straight back to work. And I think that's a result of many years of them just being super-focused, and not getting too high, but at the same time, not getting too low when the losses come." After her final Wimbledon match, "they said, 'I'm proud of you.' That was all I needed."[54]

She started playing tennis at five years old.

So, the 'overnight sensation' had been working on her tennis for 13 years, quietly behind the scenes.

She had paid the price.

Success beckoned, and nature finally gave up the object of her 13-year struggle.

The US Open 2021.

I have used Emma Raducanu in this section because she embodies the essence of paying the price of success.

It also reinforces my belief that some principles work in all fields if they are applied correctly. It's the reason why sport icons such as Sir Alex Ferguson

---

54 Ibid; https://www.vogue.co.uk/arts-and-lifestyle/article/emma-raducanu-interview

and Matthew Syed have become bestselling authors and consultants and have crossed over into business, even after leaving active sports.

Like the two sides of a coin, paying the price for success come in two ways: the "controllables" and the "uncontrollables."

At the beginning of a football match, the referee calls together the captains of the opposing teams to decide which side of the pitch they will play on. He flips a coin. Heads or tails? The team that chooses heads and wins the flip gets to decide which side of the field they will play on. The ones that come up tails make do with the other side.

Heads = controllables.
Tails = uncontrollables.

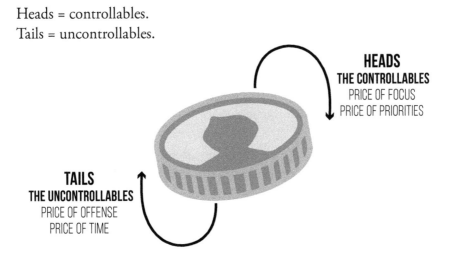

HEADS
THE CONTROLLABLES
PRICE OF FOCUS
PRICE OF PRIORITIES

TAILS
THE UNCONTROLLABLES
PRICE OF OFFENSE
PRICE OF TIME

Stephen Covey, in his iconic book *The Seven Habits of Highly Effective People*, talks about the circle of influence and the circle of concern.

The circle of influence names the parts of your success you can directly control. This is the price that YOU choose to pay. This will be equivalent to heads on the obverse side of a coin.

The circle of concern names the parts of your success you cannot control. This is the price you HAVE to pay. This will be equivalent to tails on the reverse side of the coin.

The key principle here is the following:
You set the price. Or you're set by the price.

When something is set, it means that its essential parameters are unchangeable.

My daughter and wife like to bake. The ingredients, recipe, heat of the oven, and the time to bake are all within the control of the baker. It's crucial that the baker gets it right. Once it enters the oven and it comes out, it's already set, and there is little that can be done to change the outcome.

The key is to maximise the price you pay for the controllables and minimise the time you pay for the uncontrollables.

Oh, and one more thing.

As I have stated repeatedly in this book, you cannot pay the price if you don't have enough dosh in the bank.

So it's imperative that you grab the Honeymoon Period with both hands. Store it, bank it, treasure it, save it. It's the currency you will need here in the Formative Period.

Based on the distinction between the Controllables and Uncontrollables, I have listed four prices to pay for success. Two of these are controllable. The other two are uncontrollable and are a direct consequence of the Controllables, just like Newton's Third Law or flipping a coin.

1. **The Controllables:**
    a. The Price of Focus
    b. The Price of Priorities
2. **The Uncontrollables:**
    a. The Price of Offence
    b. The Price of Time

FLIPPING THE COIN
THE CONTROLLABLES

THE PRICE OF FOCUS

Tryna find my place, find my lane, I got circus fever
The more I see, the more I feel outta place..
But sometimes I'm stressing
It's like it's never-ending…
….Feels like I'm everywhere and nowhere…

- Guvna B, "Everywhere + Nowhere," *Everywhere + Nowhere,* 2020

Would you allow an illiterate, un-schooled man off the street to perform an amputation on your son who had just returned from war or obstetrical surgery on your wife?

I didn't think so.

1984.

No, this is not the about the famous novel written by George Orwell.

It was the year which, in my humble opinion, one of the greatest feats of medicine was achieved.

And it was initiated by a little-known doctor and politician in a desperately poor African country in the midst of a crippling and devastating civil war.

Dr. Pascoal Mocumbi, Minister of Health of Mozambique.

The year was 1983, and the civil war in Mozambique had devastating effects on the country and showed no signs of slowing down. Even though the war was primarily fought by opposing Mozambicans, it was greatly exacerbated by the ever-present dark spectre of Cold War politics. It had devastated much of the Portuguese colony's infrastructure, including hospitals, rail lines, roads, and schools. This had considerably worsened an already perilous health and human resources exodus from the country, one that began after Mozambique gained independence from Portugal in 1975, leaving behind just 80 doctors to serve a country of 14 million people.

He writes:

> There was a major unmet need for emergency healthcare and life-saving skills in rural areas of Mozambique, with the biggest problems being obstetric emergencies and war casualties. Women in particular were amongst the most affected. There was an unacceptable death toll and disability from pregnancy-related complications and injuries derived from accidents and violence, among which countless women and girls suffered the health consequences of gender-based violence, harmful traditional practices, war and civil conflict.[55]

Dr. Mocumbi, who then was the Minister of Health, was faced with a conundrum. War casualties were mounting daily, and infant mortality at that time was one of the highest in the world.

Faced with an impossible situation, Dr. Mocumbi decided to train non-medical technicians to perform emergency surgical care, so he initiated an intensive, focused three-year training program to ensure technicians could become effective surgeons and perform a wide range of elective and emergency surgeries in rural areas throughout war-torn Mozambique.

They were called técnicos de cirurgia and were assistant medical officers trained for surgery in Mozambique.

---

55 Omaswa & Crisp (ed) African Health Leaders – Making Change and Claiming the Future (Oxford, Oxford University Press) Pg 181-185

Dr. Mocumbi faced intense opposition from trained nurses and doctors and paradoxically, but perhaps unsurprisingly, from surgical practitioners.

However, the death and casualty toll was mounting, and the critics had no better solutions to this controversial but necessary innovation, so the training continued, and over 110 técnicos de cirurgia were trained and deployed throughout Mozambique.

Since then, numerous studies have been published in peer-reviewed journals which have looked at the work of the técnicos over the 40-odd years the first graduates "rolled off the production line."

Fast forward to 2007.

Over the course of the year, 92 percent of all caesarean sections, obstetric hysterectomies, and laparotomies for ectopic pregnancies were performed by técnicos de cirurgia.[56]

It's not just the quantity, but the quality.

A study conducted over 15 years, assessing perceptions of standard of care provided by found that 90 percent of doctors, including surgeons, obstetricians, traumatologists, and other healthcare workers, rated their care to be good.

Another study, which was probably more astounding, found there was no clinically significant difference in post-operative outcomes between surgical operations undertaken by técnicos de cirurgia and those performed by medically qualified doctors. Post-operative mortality rates for over 10,200 patients operated on by the técnicos de cirurgia were extremely low, at 0.4 percent for emergency surgeries and 0.1 percent for elective procedures.[57]

---

56 Kruk ME, Pereira C, Vaz F, Bergstrom S, Galea S. Economic evaluation of surgically trained assistant medical officers in performing major obstetric surgery in Mozambique. British Journal of Obstetrics and Gynaecology 2007; 114: 1253-60
57 Vaz F, Bergstrom S, Vaz ML, Langa J, Bughalo A. Training medical assistants for surgery. Bulletin World Health Organisation 1999; 77:689-91

Another study looked at cost-effectiveness.

Of the 59 doctors that were trained and assigned to district hospitals in 1987, 1988, and 1996, the study revealed that none of them were still at post seven years after their training, whilst all 34 técnicos de cirurgia were still at their post.[58]

This has now become commonplace in developed nations, where paramedics, nurses, and pharmacists routinely diagnose, prescribe, and administer medicines—a discipline previously reserved for medical doctors. Dr. Mocumbi wrote:

> It is interesting to note that, as other more developed countries experience their own crises in meeting the health needs of their populations, there is growing interest globally in our experiences deploying non-physician clinicians to meet the needs of our population.

How is this relevant? Though he may not fit our 'classical' definition of one (and I bet he may not see himself as one either), Dr. Pascoal Mocumbi is every inch an entrepreneur as much as Steve Jobs or Richard Branson.

In a midst of a very uncertain environment and outcome, he has arguably started a movement, replicated in various forms across the world, from Ethiopia to the United Kingdom, and right out of the pages of *The Lean Startup* by Eric Ries.

He achieved this by the power of focus in a very uncertain and unpredictable environment.

So, basically the tecnicos de cirurgia are indicative of the price of focus because they perform highly accurate, specialised procedures due to their highly specialised, pinpoint, focused training.

---

58 Pereira C, et al. Meeting the need for emergency obstetric care in Mozambique: work performance and history of medical doctors and assistant medical officers trained for surgery. *British Journal of Obstetrics and Gynaecology 2007;* 114:1530-3

They have paid the price of focus.

In football, I have noticed one thing about the great strikers in their late 30s who keep banging in the goals. Their game becomes more and more focused on one thing. Ronaldo, Cavini, Ledadownski. They spend 90 percent of their time moving, hopping, hovering, sniffing, standing, waiting for that pass, conserving their energy for that one dash, sprint, kick that puts the ball in the back of the net.

Regarding the evergreen Christiano Ronaldo, the world's first football billionaire and still scoring prolifically at the ripe age of 37, *Sky Sports* writer Paul Merson commented:

> He's not going to close full-backs down, and he played a lot of what I would call wall passes where he just came and kept it ticking over....he's not the same player (he was in 2009 when he left for Real Madrid), but if you put the ball in the box or you look up and find him on the ball, his movement is absolutely scary...on a different level.[59]

Focus on one thing. For Ronaldo, it's putting the ball in the net. That's it. Everything else is secondary. And the older he has become, the more he's had to focus on being a striker.

But to be able to focus efficiently with results, you must make sure what you're focused on is exactly what you need to be focused on. That you're not barking up the wrong tree.

This is where validation comes in.

---

59 https://newsparho.com/cristiano-ronaldos-second-debut-for-man-utd-against-newcastle-assessed-football-news/

VALIDATION—THE KEY TO FOCUS

As Guy Raz puts it in *How I Built This,*

> When growth begins to accelerate, it's even more critical to know who you are as a founder and who you are as a company. That understanding helps point you in the right direction when you have opportunities to pursue lots of different things. It's a constant reminder of what business you're actually in, which is something that is surprisingly easy to forget or lose sight of once your business starts to expand, evolve, and change shape.[60]

This is very much the case in Africa. During my travels in my involvement in hundreds of deals across the continent, I found it easy to get caught up in the great needs and opportunities that came toward me, certainly in the healthcare sector.

It's so easy to be "***Everywhere + Nowhere.***"

I've seen promising African entrepreneurs who have ended up bankrupt, have faced criminal charges, or have lost everything because they lost focus.

The bigger the business becomes, the more opportunities get thrown at you, but to build lasting success, the more focused you need to be.

This is the case when things are going badly and you're tempted to jump ship, but, paradoxically, even more so when things are going well and opportunities are coming to you left, right, and centre.

The single most important thing you can grasp in success is focus, and you will never realise your potential unless you are prepared to focus. It's incredible what you can achieve if you do.

---

60 Raz, Guy. How I Built This – The Unexpected Paths to Success from the World's Most Inspiring Entrepreneurs (London, MacMillan, 2020)

I have painfully turned down several quick fix opportunities, some of them clearly unethical, but some way beyond my realm of expertise because of focus. I can't say it's always led to the right outcome—like my partners recently closing a $20 million agriculture deal in West Africa after I had turned it down. Oops.

But I knew, in the long run, it would stretch me too thin, and I would not be able to cope, which meant I would have to drop the pie in reaching for the apple.

So once again, validate yourself in the Honeymoon Period and stick to the knitting.

Validation is so important, so crucial, so necessary, that even though I've mentioned it in the Honeymoon Period, and again here, I'll expand on it further down this section under the Price of Time.

But you can only validate and focus once you have established your priorities, both privately and in your business.

THE PRICE OF PRIORITIES

He that lets
the small things bind him
leaves the great
Undone behind him.

- Piet Hein, "Small Things and Great"

Closely related to the price of focus is the price of priorities.

I've summarised the price of priorities this way:

1. **Banish the Bad**
2. **Let Go of the Good**
3. **Embrace the Excellent**

Banish the Bad
My weight has suddenly ballooned in the last month.

I blame my sweet tooth and the new delicious popping cherry dairy milk chocolate that has just been unleashed onto the UK market by Cadbury! I have also started to notice myself using the familiar excuse—I suffer from a chronic condition that keeps me from exercising.

But that's what it is—an excuse.

I've suffered this same condition for over a decade, and it's never stopped me from my normal 20-mile-a-week run.

As a black African whose parents both have had strokes and blood pressure issues, and who is well into middle age, I know that if it goes unchecked, I will end up with major health issues.

My bad personal decisions will inevitably spill over into my corporate life.

I'm inviting Red Flag Pain.
I talked about Red Flag Pain earlier in this book. That's a personal example of banishing the bad.

Another bad to banish is decisions, environments, and other things that run against the grain of ethics. Again, this is covered earlier in the book.

In his book, *The Power of Resilience: How the Best Companies Manage the Unexpected,* Yossi Sheffi talks about active investment detection, prevention, and response to build resilience to risks. He gives the example of Cisco:

> Rather than wait for executives to hear the news during the morning drive to work, Cisco's incident-monitoring process runs 24/7, with personnel around the world in different time zones. Cisco combines monitoring with an escalation process that guarantees a two-hour response time. During the 2011 Japan earthquake, for instance, that occurred at 9:46 Cisco headquarters local time, the company

detected an understood the significance of the event within 40 minutes and had escalated it to senior management 17 minutes later.[61]

Banishing the bad means being continually on the lookout for risks at a personal level **as well as a corporate level**. For instance, Red Flag Pain or putting **active** measures in place to detect risks from potentially derailing you as an entrepreneur or the company you are building. Doing these things costs time and money—a price. I mentioned the money I had to spend downloading the Covenant Eyes software onto all my devices—which actively monitors for pornographic content and sends messages to four carefully selected accountability partners I have chosen to alert if I begin to lapse. This, in large part, has kept me clean since 2016.

Like Cisco, we have to make sure we are continually scanning our own lives. We need to continually be on the lookout for emotions that act as triggers for Red Flag Pain. In my case, I use the acronym HALT, which I've found incredibly useful to defeat my particular Red Flag Pain every time:

Hurt
Angry
Lonely
Tired

Those are my personal four triggers which, left unchecked, will lead me down to Red Flag Pain. You have to nail down what yours are and recognise them before the gun gets loaded.

Practising the habit of recognising triggers and dealing with them before they get us develops resilience.

"Resilience—developing prevention measures, response alternatives, and detection systems—costs money, which seems to imply a choice between

---

61 Sheffi, Yossi *The Power of Resilience, How the best Companies, Manage the Unexpected* (Massachusetts, The MIT Press 2015)

fragile efficiency and expensive robustness," Yossi Sheffi writes. He talks about being risk-versed, not risk averse,[62] meaning that the more we seek growth, both in our personal lives as entrepreneurs and CEOs and in the companies we are building, the more we need to develop our sensory antennae even more to **proactively** banish the bad.

Detect, Prevent, Respond. So for me, my other potential red flag is my sweet tooth.

So when I enter the supermarket, I need to know where the chocolates, biscuits, and sweets aisle is (detect), wheel my kinetic energy in the opposite direction (prevent), and politely say no when a client brings in a box of chocolates (respond).

Plan ahead with your head to banish the bad.

Let Go of the Good
It's amazing how things pop up from the most unexpected places when you lend your ear to listening.

I was watching a famous woman just last night. She was in her late sixties.

She was a brilliant pianist and had even played for Queen Elizabeth.

She started learning how to play when she was just three years old and could read music before she could read. She played the piano diligently every day, taught by her grandmother until she was 15 years old, when she entered the University of Denver.

She had a dream of playing before the biggest audiences in the world.

But at 17 years, in 1971, she entered the summer music school at the Aspen Music Festival and realised one thing.

---

62 Ibid; Pg 367-368

She listened to a girl, the same age as her, who played a piece on the piano by ear that had taken her a whole year to learn.

She realised that she would never be good enough to be counted among the best.

So she did the unthinkable.

She threw away 13 years of her life's work as an aspiring pianist and chose to dream a new dream.

She returned to the University of Denver and almost stumbled into an international relations class with a focus on the Soviet Union.

That day, she felt something fire up in her she had never felt in the 17 years prior.

It was called passion, and it fuelled a complete turn of direction.

And she applied that same diligence she brought to the piano. Instead of being known as a world-famous pianist, she became a world-famous stateswoman and diplomat.

Secretary of State Condoleezza Rice.

The first African American to be the Secretary of State in the United States.

Yes, a brilliant pianist, but arguably, one of the most successful Secretary of States in the history of the United States.

She let go of the good to become the best.

Letting go of the good to focus on the best has been one of my greatest challenges as an entrepreneur. It cost me countless opportunities because in the scramble to land your first deal, everything goes, and you end up trying to chase everything to make that buck.

That's worsened by the fact that, by nature, I am very disorganised. I am terrible with details, get easily distracted, and am always trying to please everyone.

I remember when I had to turn down a potentially lucrative contract to source syringes from a supplier in India so as to fulfil a tender for supply in the United Kingdom. It was hard, but I did it. My client was upset. So was I. Still, I knew that wasn't my passion or purpose. It was just a distraction.

So with one eye on the prize, we need to constantly evaluate what comes our way—do we banish? Let go? Or do we embrace?

If you've done your homework well in the Honeymoon Period, knowing what to do would not be a difficult decision.

It's having the guts and discipline to "just do it."

Embrace the Excellent
It's not enough to just banish the bad and let go of the good. We must now embrace the excellent. And give it our 100 percent.

But how do we do this?

By giving it our best—focus, attention, priority, discipline, and hard work.

And yes, by learning to say no, so you can say yes.

It means we need to take a good hard look at what we stand for, what our businesses stand for, where our true priorities lie, and be prepared to go to great lengths to choose just what we need.

And choosing becomes even more acute when time is of the essence.

I once read about the story of the rocks.

A child gathered rocks and stones of various sizes and shapes, some large, some medium, some small, some tiny, along with a lot of sand on the beach.

She was given a large glass container and challenged to fill it with those rocks.

First, she randomly placed all the rocks and sand into the container.

That didn't work.

Then she tried beginning with the small ones, then adding the medium and large ones.

That didn't work either.

Then a wise old man came by and asked her to try starting with the biggest ones first.

So she placed the biggest rocks into the vase first.

Then the medium ones.

Then the small ones.

Then the tiny ones.

Then the sand.

Suddenly, the vase seemed bigger.

There was even space to add water at the end.

The same applies to our lives and business.

You need to work out your priorities from your Honeymoon Period—both in your personal life and your business—and devote time to them first. You can use WGLL to make these determinations.

Your priorities are your big rocks, your *excellents*. The ones you embrace.

Then you will find that you have space for the other less important things and so on.

And the earlier you start this process, the bigger your vase will be. The less time you have, the more excellents you have to embrace, the more good you have to let go, and the more ruthless you have to be about banning the bad.

The list of the excellents grows smaller and smaller, and the bad grows bigger and bigger.

That's how Davide Rebellin is still at the top of his game in cycling at the age of 50. Davide was the first athlete to win all three Ardennes Classics—the Amstel Gold Race, Liège–Bastogne–Liège, and La Flèche Wallonne within a week.

He has over 60 successes during a 30-year career and is still one of the finest in the sport.

Does he have any secrets to his longevity? No, none apart from passion, love, an inhuman amount of training, and a simple life: In an interview with BBC Sport last September (2021), he said:

> My wife and I feel the benefits of a regular, simple life: at home, we get up at 6:30, do some muscle toning, get a good breakfast. Then I am about on my bike at around 9:30 a.m. I eat a light meal when I'm back. Then we take dinner at around six and go to bed at nine. [63]

---

63 https://www.bbc.co.uk/sport/cycling/58317954

At 50, he is still at the top of this game, and is racing—and beating—the sons of his former competitors.

He has embraced the excellent: his wife, his nutrition, and his cycling.

That's it.

Everything else has taken a backseat.

It is what entrepreneur and author Brian Scudamore, in his *USA Today* and Amazon-bestselling book *BYOB*, terms as availability bias:

> Availability bias is the cognitive bias that focuses on the pleasure of eating the marshmallow immediately… Successful people are the ones who have figured out how to distract themselves from the concrete, short-term pleasure of eating the marshmallow and focus on an abstract, longer-term reward.[64]

And this applies for every scenario. The business decisions you have to take. Keeping yourself in top shape to forsake that cake. Having the balls to make the right calls. Who to have lunch or brunch with. The relationships to make or to forsake.

Which brings us to the next price I want to talk about.

---

64 Scudamore, Brian. BYOB: Build Your Own Business and Be Your Own Boss (Lioncrest Publishing, 2022)

FLIPPING THE COIN
THE UNCONTROLLABLES

THE PRICE OF OFFENCE

I got a body but I lost my mind
I'm just business
Placeholder with a bottom line
I'm just business

Please don't take this personally
It's just business

I need you to be wrong...
You need me to be wrong... (all along we both were wrong)

- Switchfoot, "I Need You (to Be Wrong)," *Interrobang*, 2021

Offence is one of those strange things in business. You are either giving it or taking it. There's no middle ground.

Offence. It's a price you will pay regardless of whether you choose to or not.

Ben Horowitz, in his brilliant book *The Hard Thing About Hard Things*, says that under stress and struggle, CEOs make one of the following two mistakes—they either take things too personally or they do not take things personally enough.[65]

How true that is.

In taking things too personally, we take offence.

---

65 Horowitz, Ben. *The Hard Thing about Hard Things* (New York, Harper Collins Business, 2014)

In not taking things personally enough, we find ourselves afraid to offend.

Flipping the coin.

Let's dive in, shall we?

Taking Offence

When speaking about the Honeymoon Period, we mentioned identity as something crucial to cultivate. Having stable and enduring self-confidence comes from learning to separate your performance from your self-worth.

This is where it gets serious. If we don't separate who we are from what we do, we will easily take things too personally and wreck the train.

There is something about working in Africa that makes these things all too real.

I don't know whether it's to do with the images on TV of starving children with houseflies swirling around their mouths like the earth orbiting the sun, what we read in the press, the inferiority complex that Africans face, or the rampant corruption in some parts of the continent, but I have continually had to fight taking offence and keep my eyes on the bigger picture.

I remember when a partner came to me excited with what she thought was a brilliant deal.

"So, I met a guy who is a huge guy in waste management," she said. "He is planning on setting up massive landfill sites all over Africa for Europe, North America, South America, to transfer their waste. He's tied up with several European governments that don't want waste to be dumped within Europe. His plan is to make Africa the landfill region for the world."

She couldn't understand why I was incredulous. But she must have felt a twinge in her soul because she questioned the ethics. His reply sent my blood boiling and my heart rate through the roof.

"Rest assured—these guys need the pennies we throw at them. These are the poorest people, and eventually in capitalism, the poor are employed as labour, in this case, as dumping zones for the rest of the world. Without our money, they'll starve to death or sell their souls or do something desperate."

Remember the slave trade?

My anger was not just at this businessman trying to make a buck, but at least equally the greedy African leaders who had also accepted to dump waste on their soil for money when every other continent had refused.

I realised that this partner of mine needed education because she was coming at it with a good heart. So I turned my offence into a 30-minute diatribe on why this was a bad deal.

She realised and understood. But, I'm sorry to say, the allure of thousands of dollars of easy money was too hard to turn down. I was extremely disappointed, but not surprised.

I could tell you story after story of people who feel they can screw you over, with the expectation that you will accept whatever crumbs fall from your table just because you're African, and you're desperate.

And if you're not careful and take offence, you simply can throw the baby out with the bathwater. We nearly did when a partner offered us a paltry percentage of a $15 million agriculture deal and we said no, or when we came across information about what our non-African partners really thought about us.

Mind you, it cuts both ways. My subtle inferiority complex sometimes made me make some cutting remarks, made me say some things that didn't have to be said.

Of course, you call out ignorance and stupidity when you see it. But there is a time, a manner, and a place.

It's an uphill battle.

I've used examples from my life to illustrate the point.

In reality, it could be anything. People trying to cheat you because you're a woman, disabled, or because they perceive you to be weak. It could be greed, ignorance, or selfishness.

It's easy to take it personally.

I like how Ben Horowitz put it:

> Focus on the road, not the wall.

In other words, keep your eyes and focus on the destination. If you focus on the road, you will follow the road. If you focus on the wall, you will wreck the car. Keep your eyes on the endgame.

Having said that, every attack on you has some truth to it. It's your responsibility to sit back, swallow (gulp!) the pride, take out the kernel of truth, and apply it to your life. You may have to do some digging, and sometimes the kernel may be on the tiny side, but it's always there.

Of course, it doesn't mean you have to be a doormat, but be a bridge. See the bigger picture. Keep your eyes on the prize.

Swat away the annoying flies that try to get in the way. It's difficult and nerve-wracking, but that's what you signed up for when you decided to be an entrepreneur, right? Focus on the destination. You'll enjoy the journey much more if you do.

Giving Offence

In my roles, both as a consultant community pharmacist for the NHS and as an investment consultant in BlueCloud, I have realised one thing when working with people.

You will always offend people, whether you act or whether you don't. That's why I've listed offence as an uncontrollable.

You give offence, for example, when you don't take things personally enough and you act to solve basic issues with an optimism that is extremely naive and unthinking. Or perhaps you're so afraid of upsetting people that you delegate the difficult decisions of confronting basic problems—trying to be the good cop all the time.

You either act or you will be acted upon. As an entrepreneur, you have to learn to face opposition. It's part of the game plan, the occupational hazard.

You either set the price, or it will be set for you.

I have the same tendency to make everybody happy, but it's impossible.

Of course, the opposite is also true—we all know of the gung-ho boss who comes in charging like a bull in a china shop and upsets everyone over the slightest issues.

Ultimately, after a lot of personal reflection, I came to realise that the key to handling the price of offence lies with the 3 C's: courage, character, and compassion.

Character is the underlying attribute, the foundation. It upholds courage and compassion.

Character
I have heard many definitions of character.

"The mental and moral qualities distinctive to an individual."—Oxford English Dictionary[66]

---

66 https://www.oxfordlearnersdictionaries.com/definition/american_english/character

"The real you when no one is looking."—NF[67] and Charles Swindoll[68]

"The attributes or features that distinguish an individual."—Merriam-Webster[69]

Whilst all of this is true, and there is more than a little overlap with the principles of ethical entrepreneurship, my favourite definition is from Dr. Henry Cloud:

"Character is simply the ability to meet the demands of reality."[70]

We tend to see a lack of character as a moral failure, losing the moral compass, or as a lack of principles exhibited in behaviours like dishonesty, stealing, or having an affair.

Not always so.

Dr. Henry Cloud explains further:

> "Who a person is will ultimately determine if their brains, talents, competencies, energy, effort, deal-making abilities, and opportunities will succeed."[71]

So whilst our ethics are a part of our character, they're not the whole picture. Dr. Cloud explains the most important tool is ultimately the person and his or her makeup, but paradoxically, that seems to require the least amount of attention and work. So even though many leaders meet the standards of ethical integrity, they fall short in six areas:

1. Gaining the complete trust of the people they're leading
2. Seeing all the realities of what they are facing
3. Given their talents, resources, and abilities, actually working in a way that produce the outcomes expected

---

67 NF, Remember This, Perception, 2020. (See The Pay The Price Spotify Playlist for the full lyrics)
68 Swindoll, Charles: Hand me Another Brick, (Nashville, Bantam Books, 1978)
69 Merriam-webster relevant definition of character https://www.merriam-webster.com/dictionary/character
70 Cloud, Henry. Integrity: The Courage to meet the demands of reality (New York, HarperCollins, 2006) Pg 24
71 Ibid; Pg 8-9

4. Dealing with problem people, negative situations, failures, setbacks, and losses
5. Creating growth in all aspects of the organisations where they work
6. Transcending their own interests and becoming part of a larger mission[72]

Do you have the ability within yourself to confront issues when they arise? To take things personally enough? To start from who?

This is your business. You've put in the hard work, the grind, the "blood, toil, sweat, and tears" as Winston Churchill called it.

You can either watch it begin to crumble before your very eyes or take necessary steps to ensure its survival and success. And this almost always involves making difficult decisions.

To confront, you must accept your vulnerability as a fallible person, but have enough inner strength and integrity to take on the problem regardless. There is a difference between a hypocrite and a coward.

A hypocrite is one who ignores the huge deficits of character in his own life but is quick to point out the shortcomings of others.

A failing department? A disruptive manager? An unreliable supplier? Make sure you're not one yourself.

On the other hand, your internal struggles, fears, and vulnerabilities should not stop you short from confronting destructive behaviours in others when you notice them.

That is when you start to become a coward.

We all are prone to acting with cowardice or hypocrisy.

---

72 Ibid, pg 9

People are not looking for perfection —we all know it doesn't exist. But people will follow a leader who is working on his own issues.

Both the coward and the hypocrite lack character, but character is just the foundation. On top of character lies two other crucial attributes, courage and compassion.

Courage

Courage is doing it scared.

In fact, I define courage as the sum of **intention** and **action.**

The work of the critic is easy. Spot the problem.

The work of the CEO, founder, or entrepreneur is tough. Spot the problem, devise a solution, and then do something about implementing it.

Doing something requires courage.

In my native Ghanaian dialect, Akan, courage is loosely translated as "medicine for the heart." As I reflected on this translation during a recent morning run, it struck me how true it is. A lot of the diseases we face are caused by stress, worry, and fear. Courage really is medicine for the heart. We all feel much better when we do what we know needs to be done.

And not doing so sometimes has disastrous consequences.

I once worked for a few years with a small-business owner who did not have this attitude. He owned a chain of small retail health shops spread across different towns throughout the south of England.

He was a nice man. Very polite, dignified, professional. He was honest, a fantastic father, and a great husband.

There was something I remember distinctively about him. His smile.

He seemed to genuinely care about his employees. And we got on really well.

But there was a steady stream of people leaving the organisation all the time, bitter, twisted, and hurt. Everyone who left had nothing nice to say about him. And I mean everyone. Without exception. I'm talking about scores of employees representing different backgrounds, professions, genders, and ages.

At first, I couldn't reconcile my impressions of him with this fact. It seemed like an oxymoron, a paradox.

But it came to me years later when I joined that exodus.

People were frustrated, bitter, and angry not because of him as a person, but because of his failure to personally act when tough decisions had to be made.

Instead of grabbing the bull by the horns and making the tough call when tough calls had be made, he hid behind emails, WhatsApp messages, texts, tweets and "delegation" to deliver bad news. Of course, he would show up and smile when there was good news.

The paradox was the smile that attracted people to him eventually drove them away.

And this failure to act had serious consequences. A pending court case on accusations of bullying as well as accusations of racism. Upset customers left in droves amidst infighting and abuse.

He smiled employees in, and he smiled employees out.

He reminded me of the 2003 comedy *Bruce Almighty* with Jim Carrey and Morgan Freeman. Bruce (Jim Carrey) is given the opportunity to play God by Morgan Freeman's character. Eventually, in the face of an overwhelming number of requests from human beings, Bruce is shown saying 'yes to all.' Needless to say, extreme chaos results.

This CEO had a lack of courage.

He saw the problems because he was constantly being reminded of them. They were staring him in the face.

He knew the solutions, but he lacked the inner courage to do them.

So the exodus continued and still does to this day. The businesses continue to suffer and people continue to leave.

And he still continues to smile.

Compassion

He tells her that the earth is flat—
He knows the facts, and that is that.
In altercations fierce and long
She tries her best to prove him wrong.
But he has learned to argue well.
He calls her arguments unsound
And often asks her not to yell.
She cannot win. He stands his ground
The planet goes on being round.

- Wendy Cope, "Differences of Opinion"

Reflecting on the last two years, it's amazing how entrenched the world has become in polarized views. Brexit versus Remain, Republicans versus Democrats, vaccine advocates and anti-vaxxers.

It seems we are lacking the ability to really listen and learn from each other. There's no doubt that we live in an increasingly divisive time where our fossilised and calcified opinions are tearing us apart.

That's why it's refreshing that the recent study done by the respected Development Dimensions International showed empathy to be the biggest single leadership skill needed today.

The finding reflects assessments of more than 15,000 leaders in 18 countries. The survey also found that the top ten performing businesses in the 160 studies the Institute conducted generated 50 percent more net income than the bottom ten performers.

But empathy is not all.

We need to go beyond empathy to compassion.

So for the purposes of this book, I define compassion as the sum of **empathy** and **action**.

While empathy refers more generally to our learned ability to take the perspective of and feel the emotions of another person, compassion goes beyond mere feelings to concrete steps and actions that put empathy into practice.

When confronting any issue, we need to focus, not on settling scores or pursuing a narrow crusade, but on removing any semblance of rot that may threaten the future success of the organisation.

Practically speaking, listening and striving to understand where the other person is coming from is crucial if you are to reap the changed behaviour that would lead to success. According to Muhammad Sajwani, founder at Evolve HR, when done right, empathy plus action are likely to lead to the following five desirable outcomes. Interestingly, these outcomes are a direct result of employees feeling like they are part of the organisation:

1. Better employee retention
2. Better employee engagement
3. Better internal collaboration
4. Better job satisfaction
5. Enhanced innovation

So, don't just end at empathy—continue with compassion.

THE PRICE OF TIME

That is a strange day
when you wake to discover
Age has drifted down
imperceptibly, like dust
And you're totally covered.

- Alan Hill, "That Is a Strange Day"

Time

Under "Pain," I talked about Amber Flag Pain, meaning the pain of a mismatch between the entrepreneur and the market.

The only solution is to reorient, keep working, and wait.

What I didn't mention is *how long* the waiting process would be. It's a bit illusory to use the amber traffic light as an analogy, because with amber, you have to wait for only a matter of seconds before the traffic light turns green and you can go.

It's what I have chosen to call the **weight** of the **wait.**

The burden of time.

What if I told you the wait could last for at least a decade? Could you still hold on? Time is a price we all have to pay.

Through history, we've been fascinated by the number 10.

We name generations based on what decade they were born in—baby boomers, millennials, Gen Z, Gen Y.

We talk about music of the 60s, 70s, 80s, and 90s.

We talk about a perfect 10. We measure big milestone birthdays in 10s after the 20th year. This occurred to me after I joined in the 50th birthday celebrations of a fellow friend and entrepreneur.

I mentioned at the beginning of this book that 90 percent of businesses fail after 10 years.

I couldn't agree more with British podcaster and millionaire Steven Bartlett, who, in his *Diary of a CEO* podcast, says that we must be willing to commit at least a decade to see the sustained success of any business.

So, would it be so strange if the Amber Flag Pain wait could last for up to ten years? Would you have such belief and faith in your Honeymoon Period that you could stick it out for ten years?

Idris Ayodeji Bello did.

Idris is a founding partner at LoftyInc Capital Management, a pan-African VC firm. After 12 years of trying, on 31 August, 2021, LoftyInc finally launched its biggest fund yet, a $10 million fund for tech startups in Africa.

Now, $10 million may seem like a tiny sum in the VC world, where funds raised are counted in the billions, not millions.

Paradoxically, it can be far more difficult to raise a fund in the tens of millions than to raise one in the billions because investors come up with the same line:

"What's the point? It costs the same amount in time and money to do due diligence for a medium-sized company as it does for a multi-million-dollar company. And the rewards are so much better for the latter."

And yes, he could raise more. Lots more. But in Africa, the problem is deployment. Very few startups and companies are at the stage where they could absorb capital of more than $500,000.00.

"My approach for raising funds is different," he said to me on our conference call. "I like to start organically—I feel that once you get up to $50-100 million, then the problem arises on how to deploy the funds, especially in Africa—where very few startups and funds can handle capital of more than a few hundred thousand pounds at a time."

Idris didn't have to roll up his sleeves this way; he had other choices.

He had a comfortable life working at Chevron and Exxon Mobil, as well as working with the Clinton Health Access Initiative.

A graduate of University of Houston (MBA) and Oxford (Global Public Health), he was a 2011 recipient of the Lord Weidenfeld Scholarship for demonstrating remarkable potential as a future leader from an emerging economy.

And the accolades are numerous:

Listed among CNN's Top Ten African Technology Voices, he is a Singularity University Impact Fellow, Harambean Fellow, Clinton Global Initiative University Fellow, MIT Global Startup Fellow, SAP Ashoka Global Change-makers Award Winner, Dell Technology Award Winner, StartingBloc Innovation Fellow, and Nigeria Leadership Initiative Future Leader.

But it all changed when he visited his home city of Lagos, Nigeria in 2010.

As I explained earlier on in this book, real growth potential in Africa, unlike the Western world, lies in the SME sectors, where it is hardest to raise money and where the least reward for the hardest work lies. In other words, you need to be prepared to roll up your sleeves, go for the long haul, and be prepared for multiple failures if you want to give a leg up to the numerous tech startups littered across the continent.

He realised during his return to Lagos that the next wave of innovation that Africa as a continent needed rested on the shoulders of up-and-coming founders.

So just being a plain VC firm would not work. The firm had to do all three: be a hub, a venture accelerator, and a venture arm, or, as he calls it, an enterprise development company.

What he didn't realise at the time was how long it would take.

12 years.

12 years of languishing, pain, and the loss of hundreds of thousands of dollars, a ton of mistakes, rejects, starting over, and the whole game.

That's the part the press just glosses over.

Like this quote from *TechCrunch*:

> **Bello likes to describe his 12-year venture into technology and entrepreneurship as an "Afropreneurship journey."** While in business school in the U.S., he realized that the next wave of innovation that Africa as a continent needed rested on the shoulders of up-and-coming founders.
>
> With that in mind, Bello started LoftyInc Allied Partners alongside other entrepreneurs as an enterprise development company. It spun off a technology hub and venture accelerator called Wennovation Hub, and also the venture arm called LoftyInc Capital.
>
> In 2012, the firm launched the first fund—LoftyInc Afropreneurs Fund 1—as its pre-seed-stage investment vehicle. The fund acted more like a syndicate or an angel group, of which investors includes senior executives in key industries across Africa (emphasis mine).[73]

So, what was the reality of this 12-year journey? I was keen to find out, so I caught up with him on a Zoom conference call to hear the real story of LoftyInc. It turns out it was a million miles from what the media has painted it out to be.

---

73 https://guce.techcrunch.com/copyConsent?sessionId=3_cc-session_63a2db41-5f44-4297-a1ce-3e4d462a8e21&lang=en-US

First, he visited Lagos in 2010 and tried to launch the fund.

It failed.

He tried again in 2012.

It failed.

Then in 2012 he launched the LoftyInc Afropreneur fund. He tried pitching to family offices, and high-net-worth-income holders. Again, it failed.

Then there was a period of waiting from 2012 to 2016 where he had to fall back on his paid 9-to-5. During this trial-and-error period, he lost a ton of money and was staring bankruptcy in the face.

He then tried to build angel networks as he felt that in Africa, that part of the necessary infrastructure did not exist yet. He, again, poured in a lot of effort, money and time into this. If felt like it was going nowhere.

However, his Honeymoon Period was strong. He knew exactly what the problem was and how he planned to solve it.

It was during this period that he met Marsha Wulff, an early-stage investor who had a long history of involvement with development in Africa. They met in 2010, and Marsha became an advisor to the firm, but it was another SEVEN years, in 2017, that she came on board as an anchor investor and general partner in the fund.

They then launched Fund 2, their first VC fund in 2017 in Mauritius, but didn't get much traction and ran into huge costs that forced them to abandon Mauritius and move to Delaware in the US and keep raising.

Then COVID struck.

They were forced to close the fund even though they had fallen far short of their target. It looked like all his dreams were dead in the water.

But then finally, it happened.

Finally, in July 2021, LoftyInc made headlines, and to make things even better, some of the companies they had invested in also made headlines.

One such company is Flutterwave, an African-based fintech company that provides a payment infrastructure for global merchants and payment service providers across the continent. Flutterwave was one of the initial companies LoftyInc invested in during 2016.

Now, as Idris puts it, "Everyone is knocking at the door." They can smell the money. After 12 years, they also want to follow the money.

Slowly, steadily, suddenly.

As I write this, DrugStoc, a Nigerian medicines wholesale distribution company which I mentioned earlier, finally raised $4.4 million. I met them in Lagos in 2015 when they were working out of a tiny backroom office.

It took them six years.

I like using examples from Africa because it magnifies these principles of the Honeymoon Period. In Africa, you'd better believe in what you set out to achieve and have the passion to carry it through and the research to back it up because, more likely than not, you will be in for a long haul.

But this principle holds across the world. We all see entrepreneurs (think of the social media entrepreneurs who make millions on the back of a couple of videos) who quickly rise up from nowhere. If they really did rise up from nowhere, chances are that they will also disappear into nowhere. With that said, if they'd only seemingly rose up from nowhere, but had actually been waiting in time's crucible, there will most likely be a "suddenly." That "suddenly" moment has finally come for LoftyInc Financial.

At last check in 2021, Loftyinc has invested in more than 50 startups and early-stage companies from Egypt to Pakistan, from Nigeria to the United States. And many of these companies, like Flutterwave and Reliance HMO, are now household names in the countries where they ply their trade. Others, such as Volumetric and Asalyxa Bio, are at the forefront of healthcare technology in the United States.

These principles apply universally, even outside of business.

I was recently watching the trilogy documentary of Kanye West by his loyal confidant, Coodie. I was shocked to learn that Kanye had been trying to perform and come out with his own album since he was 17 years old. He'd had success in producing beats and albums for Jay-Z, Jermaine Dupri, and many other big hitters, but nobody believed he could rap and produce for himself. He had to move from Chicago to New York and literally bang on doors for almost a decade before Roc-a-Fella Records finally decided to sign him on in 2002. His subsequent debut album, *The College Dropout*, which he released in 2004, was a massive success with domestic sales close to 3.5 million copies and certified four times platinum by the RIAA in 2020. It happened 10 years after taking the plunge.

Kanye West, Emma Raducanu, and Loftyinc have all finally made it. Their Honeymoon Period was strong, and they had enough belief in themselves and their purpose, so the Camel Principle was able to carry them through Amber Flag Pain.

Grit, perseverance, and belief in themselves, but most of all, they had paid the price of time.

Grabbing Hold of Time: The Concept of Personal Capacity

The above examples I have given may give the erroneous impression that we are helpless in the sphere of time, but this couldn't be further from the truth.

True, some things take time, but we also waste a lot of time with our action or inaction. Amber Flag Pain and the price of time must be actively maximised.

Canadian leader and motivational speaker Leon Fontaine speaks about the concept of personal capacity.

Every single human being on planet earth has a measure of personal capacity.

Your personal capacity, he maintains, determines the quality of your life, and by extension, the quality of your business.

It, along with character determines how much success you can take without "spilling the milk."

What then is this concept of personal capacity?

It is not solely determined by your education, your skills, your gifting, or your stewardship.

Leon Fontaine defines personal capacity as the following:

Personal Capacity = Ability + Resources + Stewardship.[74]

I spoke about the principle of stewardship in the five principles of ethical entrepreneurship. The resources are the means at our disposal to steward the purposes we have or the dreams we wish to realize.

But our capacity to expand will only increase with the ability that we have.

So, in the Amber Flag Pain period, we should be using the time we have to build our personal capacity and the capacity of those who we are working with so as to fulfil our vision, our mission, our dream.

---

74 https://leonfontaine.podbean.com/e/personal-capacity-determines-the-quality-of-your-life/

Any failure in our personal capacity will eventually spell doom for our company by giving rise to Red Flag Pain, where our lurking failures derail our best intentions.

Why am I speaking about this in the context of time?

Because rather than becoming worriers during the Amber Flag Pain period, we should aim to become **warriors** by building our personal capacity to handle the eventual challenges that will come with our increased resources.

10 to 12 years is a long time to wait around complaining, sulking, and doing nothing.

We should be ready when the market is ready.

But how?

May I suggest four ways?

1. Personal: invest time in expanding your personal capacity

In a refugee camp on the border of a war-torn country, a queue of thousands of adult refugees stand in line to receive their daily ration of a slice of warm bread and two ladles of nutritious, hot soup for their breakfast.

The weather is cold, the floors flooded and muddy. Anxious soldiers patrol the camp to quell disorder and keep out warring factions. Charity workers ensure there is an orderly line of people standing in line before the giant makeshift kitchen in the middle of the camp.

For the soup, children receive a ladle, teenagers two ladles, and adults three ladles. The charity does not supply containers for the soup—the refugees have to bring their own.

The camera zooms on the first few dozen or so refugees.

For the first refugee, a 29-year-old handsome male, the three ladles fill his bowl to the brim. For the next refugee, an older man, the container begins to fill up after the second ladle. After the charity worker begins to pour in the third ladle, his container overflows. Not wanting to waste the soup, the worker has to stop. The man walks gingerly away trying not to spill the precious food.

The next refugee gets out her container. She is a 40-year-old woman with a child on her back and another just behind her. The camera zooms on her. The three ladles barely fill more than half of her container.

Then there was this old man, possibly in his early seventies. His container was large and looked like it could easily fit his ration. But something strange happened.

The soup stayed at the same level, even as the worker continued to pour. It took a few moments to realise the problem.

He had a leak in his container. That man went away hungry, not because there were no resources available, but because his personal capacity was compromised. He lacked stewardship. He wasn't able to keep what was given to him.

We can think of each refugee's container as their personal capacity.

And if we don't spend time actively developing our personal capacity, we will not be able to handle the resources.

Personal Capacity = Ability + Resources + Stewardship.

Too many of us spend time chasing the resources, but not enough time working on our ability and our stewardship.

Our abilities are not just directly related to our purposes or vision. They depend on investments in our health, our fitness, and our close relationships. Though they are not directly related to the vision we have, they have the power to mitigate Red Flag Pain, which can completely derail our personal capacity. I gave my own example of this in the previous chapter.

Even in circumstances like White Flag Pain, investing in our personal capacity will give us the resilience we need when the inevitable crash happens.

Just as important, if we don't grab hold of the time to invest in the capabilities, education, skills and competencies required, it will limit our personal capacity. This involves reading, attending conferences and seminars, formal and informal study, and actively encouraging mentorship. Simply put, we must keep learning.

Investing in our stewardship competencies are also crucial. If we don't fix the leaks in our containers, we will waste a lot of unnecessary time and resources before we finally achieve our goal. Increasing our stewardship competencies means we can keep more and waste less.

My 12 years in the wilderness can be chalked up as much as my not having invested in my personal capacity as it is to the Amber Flag Pain I talked about in the example of LoftyInc Capital.

In other words, it didn't have to be 12 years in the wilderness. It could have been 10. Or eight.

So what steps can we take now to increase our personal capacity? This brings us to our next point:

2. Reflection: actively learning from mistakes, events, and developments

Even Amber Flag Pain can be an opportunity for reflection. We have the opportunity to actively learn from the mistakes we make and the events that are out of our control. The old adage and cliché stands and rings true: *whatever doesn't kill us should make us stronger.*

But this also demands our active use of time. In other words, the only thing stopping us from doing this is making the time to practice.

If we don't reflect, we are bound to make the same mistakes each time we get to a similar obstacle, which again prolongs the time we take to get to our goal.

There are two reasons why we don't reflect. We are too busy running around like headless chickens, or we feel we don't need to take time out to reflect. Perhaps we believe ourselves invincible, or we simply don't like what we see in the mirror, so we behave like the proverbial ostrich.

I see this in Bello. A man doesn't acquire so many accolades, degrees, and experiences by languishing in self-pity. His impressive résumé indicates a man who is committed to working hard at his craft, even in the face of incredible difficulties.

He used his time in the wilderness to study, network, work hard, prepare the ground, and fine-tune his research and findings, so when the inevitable success came, his personal capacity had expanded to be able to take it.

3. Corporate: investing time in expanding the capacity of our business and relationships

We can only grow as far as our regular partners, colleagues, and collaborators. We need to invest time in building their capacity, showing genuine love and concern for their welfare, both on and off the threshing ground, and expanding their horizons, wherever they are. Sometimes it may even mean expanding their capacity outside our business. But good time invested is never wasted. Whatever we invest in our colleagues, we will get back. It's an unbreakable principle, and I've seen it so many times in my own life.

4. Relaxing: learning to unwind and enjoy life during the waiting process

Life cannot be all about working and waiting. It should also be about enjoying, unwinding, and living. I touched about this earlier on in the Honeymoon Period. The tendency we have is to swing from one extreme to the other. The Amber Flag Period should also be about enjoying the journey on the way to the destination. We should learn to savour the joy of the mundane—the time with family; lunch with friends; time with the dog in the park; the brilliant sunset or sunrise by the beach; the football game at the pub or chop bar or restaurant; celebrating the small wins along the way. This makes the Amber Flag Period less arduous, more bearable, and more enjoyable. It's something we all need to learn to do more of (or less of) as the situation may be. Life is to be lived. We need to thrive, and not just survive, as I quoted earlier from the band Switchfoot.[75]

Validation Revisited: The Concept of "Stagility"

Just because you do it
Doesn't mean you always will.
Whether you're dancing dust
or breathing light
you're never exactly the same,
twice.

- Yrsa Daley-Ward, "What Will Be Will Soon Be Past"

"No strategy survives contact with reality; no strategy succeeds unchanged by reality."
- Dr. Max McKeown

In 1905, Ernest Rutherford, a New Zealand physicist, did an experiment to test the "plum pudding" model of the atom. Until this experiment, it was widely believed that positive charges and negative charges were

---

75 See associated Spotify playlist 'Pay the Price for full lyrics.

distributed evenly throughout the atom. He directed a beam of alpha particles (a form of nuclear radiation with a large positive charge) at very thin gold leaf suspended in a vacuum. Gold was used because it was the only metal that could be rolled out to be thin without cracking, and it was suspended in a vacuum so that the collisions would take place with the gold foil and nothing else. He found the following:

- Most of the particles passed straight through the foil (moving in a straight line)
- A small number of alpha particles were deflected by large angles as they passed through the foil (pivot)
- A very small number of alpha particles were repelled and came back straight off the foil (quit)

Thus, Rutherford was able to prove that the atom consisted mostly of empty space, with a small concentration of positive charges in the middle, which repelled the alpha charges.

I have adapted this model to illustrate the concept of testing validation. The radioactive source is your honeymoon-validated idea, the gold foil is reality and time, and the alpha particles are your efforts to turn that validated idea into reality:

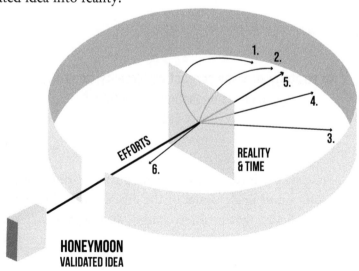

There is something that happens to us in the process of paying the price of time and after we've faced our pain. After the waiting, the suffering, the struggle, the bumping and riding, we will arrive at a point where we have to make a decision.

I heard of the concept of "stagility" (which is a combination of 'stability' and 'agility') from the book *CEO Excellence: The Six Mindsets that Distinguish the Best Leaders from the Rest.*[76]

With validation, there will need to be a balance. The validated concept with which you started before you hit the Formative Period will have to inform your decision as to what to do next. This is where you have to be stagile. Stable enough not to get swayed from your initial decision, but agile enough to know that your initial validated decision may need some tweaking, some pivoting.

Do we keep going with our original market plan, or do we adapt and/or pivot?

In my mind, there are three things that could happen: you can continue to move in a straight line, pivot, or quit.

1. **Unrelated Pivot: Temporary, Market-driven**
2. **Related Pivot: Temporary, Market-driven**
3. **Unrelated Pivot: Market-driven, Permanent**
4. **Related Pivot: Market-driven, Permanent**
5. **No Pivot: Straight Line Movement**
6. **Quit**

1. Unrelated Pivot: Temporary, Market-driven: We saw a lot of this during the COVID lockdown period when due to the strict restriction of movement, some companies had to adapt to keep. During the COVID

---

76 Dewar, Kella and Malhotra. *CEO Excellence: the Six Mindsets that Distinguish the Best Leaders from the Rest* (New York, Scribner, 2022)

pandemic, The Ministry of Health in Ghana, West Africa recommended regular handwashing with soap and running water and the use of alcohol-based rub/sanitizers in line with WHO guidelines. However, how could this be achieved in a country which, even before the pandemic, had challenges with availability of clean running water?

This problem had even become more crucial due to limited local production and delayed imports—and even though the government tried to cushion the blow by offering free water for three months, the prices of sanitizers still went through the roof.

The government had to turn to the private sector for help—and this is where Kasapreko came in.

Kasapreko, one of Ghana and West Africa's largest alcohol companies, with big plans to go global before the pandemic, suddenly found itself in a conundrum. Due to the pandemic, sales had stalled. But it saw an opportunity. The WHO had published a free formula for hand sanitizer, and an NGO, the Total Family Health Organization, worked with Kasa-preko to produce the KCL Hand Sanitizer Range. This proved extremely popular in the local Ghanaian market, alleviated the handwashing crisis, and provided a much-needed temporary income stream for Kasapreko in dire times. This was an example of a company branching into an unrelated market due to Amber Flag Pain. And it worked.

2. Related Pivot: Temporary, Market-driven: In my capacity as a consultant pharmacist working with the Wellcare Group, a small community pharmacy chain in the UK, a hitherto unknown company called Goodbody approached us with a proposition. Could we help them pilot a scheme to provide guaranteed, cost-effective PCR tests to travellers who needed to come into the UK, or leave the UK for business, family, or urgent personal travel? At the time, in July 2020, the market was rife with unreliable tests, astronomical pricing, and less-than-reliable results. There was a huge need.

At the time, Goodbody was just a small company working with independent community pharmacies to produce and distribute its high-quality CBD products. It already had excellent relations with independent community pharmacies up and down the country. It partnered with high-quality labs, trusted independent couriers, and even rail companies to provide seamless, guaranteed, cost-effective PCR testing services which have been known across the country for their reliability. That pivot gained Goodbody a £36 million profit windfall at the end of 2021, not including the desperately needed income provided for independent pharmacies, independent couriers, and labs up and down the country. Though the need for PCR and antigen tests for travel are now tailing off, that windfall has surely been a win-win for all companies involved and kept Goodbody afloat and with a renewed mandate to carry on and expand its services through retail pharmacies.

3. Unrelated Pivot: Permanent, Market-driven: The decision of Greggs, a quintessential British pastry, tea, and coffee restaurant, to collaborate with Primark, one of Britain's biggest sources of fast fashion, raised eyebrows. From February 19th, 60 Primark shops would feature a 11-piece fashion clothing piece collaboration between the two high-street giants called "Fashion with Flavour."

Weird.

Especially when sausage rolls and pasties visibly appeared next to clothes on the windows of the flagship Primark Store on London's Oxford Street—or when a load of Greggs pastries and cakes had pride of place in the display window at the Primark located in UK's city of Newcastle by a £5 tracksuit and a sporty clothing range.

But what may not be so weird is that the world's largest Primark store will now play host to the world's largest Greggs store in Birmingham, England.

So there may be a method to the madness. Seeing as Primark does not offer online shopping, it may be a way to tempt more customers into its stores.

This is the sort of diversification business books and gurus frown upon because it is littered with failures.

It may be necessary in developing countries where conglomerates have to acquire or build bases in unrelated fields to succeed. For example, I think of how FedCo, one of Ghana's biggest cocoa-buying companies, had to move into the truck haulage business to ensure its purchased cocoa got to the ports reliably.

4. **Related Pivot: Permanent, Market-driven:** When we set out to form BlueCloud, market entry was not on the menu. Neither was my becoming an author. But after multiple failures and trip-ups, as well as a prolonged decade in Amber Flag Pain, we realised that market entry was a low-hanging fruit that could put money on the table whilst we reached out for what we thought was the main prize—incubating struggling middle companies and raising funds through the Afya Fund to take them to the next level.

A decade later, market entry has now taken over the bulk of business and become a mainstay of BlueCloud and Emerald. But we know that incubation, our validated concept, remains as true as ever.

So why not do both? They are related. Companies will always want to enter the exciting African market, and Africans are becoming woker and richer, so they are able to afford more luxuries.

And writing books?

I'll leave that for you to decide.

5. **No Pivot: Straight Line Movement:** This is the ideal scenario. The Amber Flag Pain period validates, confirms, and emphasises your original idea, so after coming through the pain, your stars align, and take-off happens. The contract gets signed. The deal goes through. The investors come. Your proposal gets approved.

But even with no pivot, tweaks, turns, and adjustments are inevitable.

Lift-off.

But lift-off with a healthy dose of humility, realism, purpose.

A hardened, toughened outer skin, and a softer heart, ready to face the world.

No strategy survives contact with reality; no strategy succeeds unchanged by reality.

6. Quit: I really hope this doesn't happen, but sometimes, life happens.

Your honeymoon validation collides with reality and bounces back at you. For some reason, you decide it's not worth pursuing. The price is too great. You don't even want to pivot anymore. You decide to quit. This is what happens to nearly half of entrepreneurs in the first five years and up to 90 percent after the first decade.

And I really believe that not everyone is cut out to be an entrepreneur. If you are, you will still be standing after the Formative Period. The Formative Period is the refining fire, the testing crucible, the gold leaf in Rutherford's experiment. Every entrepreneur gets tested in the Formative Period.

But you may have bought this book because you are on the verge of quitting. If so, may I redirect you to the Camel Principle?

How strong was your Honeymoon Period?

But even if you hopefully decide to move on after validation, there is still one final trap awaiting—what I call the choke trap.

AND FINALLY, DON'T CHOKE!

Right at the edge of destiny
I choke
And tired of the constant mutiny
I poke

Through the ashes and remains
Of old battles fought
Through the losses and gains
Of new victories sought

Right at the sight of victory
I choke
And quivering, getting jittery
I poke

At the old familiar itch
Which leaves the old familiar glitch
To turn the old wheels of ignominy
Right at the cliff—the edge of destiny

- Steven N. Adjei, "Choke," *From Gory to Glory*

Consider this story inspired by a true event.

The boy was starving.

For weeks, he had been trudging with his mother through the dense patches of forest with gunfire and sounds of hand grenades far in the distance behind him.

There had been no time to stop and stare, and all he could have to eat were scraps—bites—taken from the old backpack stuck to his uncle's shoulder.

He had already lost his father to the war.

It was dark, and there was a scabby wound on his knee, which he had gotten from stumbling and falling on a piece of rock two days earlier. It had started to heal, but his mother had to continually stop him from trying to pick at it.

The boy was starving, but light was coming.

They had finally reached the border.

Across the line, they were shepherded into a building, where they met a weary-faced official who looked up at the three of them, gave the boy a smile, checked their papers, and waved them on with a thud of a stamp on his passport.

On the other side, they saw a host of families with placards. One of them had their name on. The family on the other side were beaming, opening their arms wide.

Salvation was finally here.

They got ushered into the SUV, sped on the motorway down some country lanes, and finally into a mansion that was to be his new home for the next six years.

He got in and was given a warm bath, new clothes, and a lot of fuss.

The boy was still starving, but the pain he had endured was now coming to an end.

From the kitchen, he could smell heaven.

Warm bread, chicken, rice, and vegetables—the smell wafted from the kitchen to the dining table.

Finally, a plate was set before him.

The boy was starving.

He began to ravenously eat, shoving down the mouthfuls of rice and mince down his throat with no respite.

Then the unimaginable happened.

He began to choke. Splutter. Cough.

His uncle tried back-slapping. Then water. The piece of meat wouldn't budge. His mother began to scream. The boy began to turn blue.

The host called the ambulance.

Panic.

At the hospital they finally managed to dislodge the culprit. A bone in the meat had lodged itself just below his throat.

He had survived. Again.

No one even remembered the delicious food.

At the point of satisfying this craving hunger, he had choked.

This could happen to any of us in the metaphorical sense.

After going through all the pain, the distress, the anguish, right at the end, when the finish line is in sight, many entrepreneurs and leaders choke.

The old demons of Red Flag Pain surface.

I remember when I choked right at the end of a $20 million medicine and COVID appliance supply deal to the authorities in Luanda in 2019. We lost our words, and, with them, we lost the deal.

In Lagos, in 2016, right at the end of a lucrative diagnostics deal, I choked.

Red Flag Pain returned and lodged in my throat.

Why?

I could hear that voice: "You don't belong here, Steven"—the Green Flag Pain. So I took refuge by picking at the scab of Red Flag Pain. The wound reopened and unleashed Amber Flag Pain. I had to go to the back of the queue and wait again, for a whole year. It cost me dearly. The boy lost his meal, and sadly, I lost the deal.

If you are a football fan, you can remember the choke moment Marcus Rashford had at the brink of winning the Euros for England for the first time, or in the 2010 World Cup final, when the Ghanaian football captian, Asamoah Gyan, choked on the brink of sending an African footballing nation into the semi-finals of the World Cup in South Africa for the first time.

So please don't think you've arrived when success beckons right at the end of the pain. The weight of success has a way of unravelling all the work you have done in dealing with the pain.

As my friend Brian Doyle, a senior mentor at AA, introduces himself: "I am a recovering alcoholic." Even though he hasn't touched a drink for 30 years.

As Donda West said to her son Kanye,

"You need to keep your feet on the ground and your head in the air at the same time."

So, hold steady right to the end. And don't choke, now or ever.

As Steven Pressfield puts it in his bestselling book, *The War of Art*:

> The danger is greatest when the finish line is in sight. At this point, Resistance knows we're about to beat it. It hits the panic button. It marshals one last assault and slams us with everything its got… be alert for this counterattack. Be wary at the end. Don't open that bag of wind.[77]

So, hold steady right to the end. And, as Eminem says, don't choke![78]

Learn the lessons during the Formative Period.

The Legacy Period, the period of real success, beckons.

And it is to that which we now turn.

KEY CONCEPTS:
- **The Controllables:**
  - The Price of Focus
  - The Price of Priorities
- **The Uncontrollables:**
  - The Price of Offence
  - The Price of Time
  - "Stagility"

---

77 Pressfield, Steven. The War of Art (New York. Black Irish Entertaiment. 2002)
78 Lose Opportunity—see Pay The Price Spotify Playlist for full lyrics.

QUESTIONS:

1. Where have you paid the price in your own entrepreneurial journey? What strategies have you learned from this chapter that can change your relationship to the controllables and uncontrollables in your own life?

2. We read about resilience in an earlier chapter. What can you put in place to ensure you don't choke right at the end?

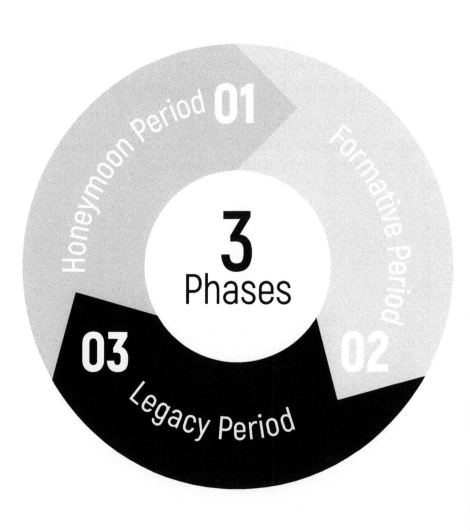

THE LEGACY PERIOD

"For you could see the way he had gone by the lights he had left behind."

- David Beresford

It was 5:34 p.m. on 18 December, 1949.

It was freezing cold in Bolton, Lancashire in the north of Britain. The day was particularly busy, and the town centre street was packed with shoppers.

No one could understand why that day was so busy.

The Market Hall, which housed independent traders, quirky shops, chain stops, and big local names, was where all the action was happening. It was impossible to hear yourself above the din of traders clamouring for their last sales, mothers screaming to their children, or the laughter of young people and factory workers hunting for bargains. It looked chaotic, but there was purpose in the chaos.

Maybe it was getting to look a lot like Christmas, or maybe it was because the hundreds of cotton mill factory workers had just been paid their December wages. Or perhaps it was both.

But the day was coming to a close, and the town centre was finally beginning to thin out. It was getting dark. As the shops were beginning to close their doors, the buses at the many bus stops were opening theirs.

But for the man in charge of the lights, the day was just beginning.

Lamplighter Anthony David Lockwood was the "lights man," as the children living in the suburb of Deansgate, Bolton called him. He was a well-respected, stately man with a slight limp as a result of an injury from the war, brown, kind eyes, and a deep baritone voice.

As his wife and four children were getting back from the city centre Bolton shops on the bus, he had just finished his supper, gotten out his equipment, and was about to head out of the door.

He had his dog, Charlie, his ladder, his wick-trimmer, and whale oil.

Setting out at 5:34 p.m., four minutes later than usual, fully dressed for the cold with his hat and coat, he took a brisk walk out in the street and started his cheery whistle. Children came out to wave to him as he started lighting up the lamps, something he had been doing for the past decade, like his father before him.

Everybody loved Anthony Lockwood.

He was a steady, trustworthy, solid man who brought some measure of reassurance and safety to the people who lived in Deansgate, especially after the depression, poverty, and pain caused by the war which had ended four years earlier.

The children said of him: "You could see the way he had gone, by the lights he had left behind."

On that tragic day, on 18 December, 1949, one of the bowls had accumulated a build-up of gas. As he climbed up the ladder to light the lamp, the built-up gas exploded and blew him off the ladder.

Anthony David Lockwood died that night.

At his funeral a week later, the vicar recalled what the children used to say about him.

The church was packed to capacity. Tears filled the eyes of almost everyone in the congregation.

By the way he had gone, both literally and metaphorically, he had left a lot of lights in the streets, the hearts, and the minds of the people of Deansgate, Bolton.

You could see the way he had gone by the lights he had left behind.

I pray for all of us, that we will leave lights behind us as we go through the maze of life.

He had left a legacy of Power and a legacy of Place.

To quote bestselling author Adam Grant,

> Too many people spend their lives being dutiful descendants instead of good ancestors.
>
> The responsibility of each generation is not to please their predecessors. It's to improve things for their offspring.
>
> It's more important to make your children proud than your parents proud.

It's more important to leave a good Power and Place Legacy.

I want to thrive, not just survive....[79]

- Switchfoot, "Thrive," *Vice Verses*, 2011

You've succeeded and gone through the Formative Period. Congratulations! You're one of the 10 percent of entrepreneurs who have survived the arduous journey. You're not looking over your shoulder anymore. You can now look forward, to the future, with relative confidence.

You've succeeded, or, rather, you're succeeding. You're now living the dream. Living what you saw in your mind's eye when you started the Honeymoon Period. You've navigated the hard bit, gotten the business off the ground, and are making money. The business is expanding.

Now, exiting the Formative Period does not mean that the company has already been formed. But we need to think of the phases as layers, which are built on top of each other, much like a multi-layered dessert.

In a way, you will never leave the Formative Period, or, should I say, businesses that truly wish to stay relevant and innovative should never leave the formative behind completely. They should always be forming, evolving, innovating, staying relevant, and ahead. But the difference here is more on focus.

It gets to the point where the focus moves to thriving and leaving a foundation where the company (and your inputs, both within and without) will continue to expand and flourish, long after you've gone.

However, with the Legacy Period, the hard work has only just begun.

Rob Dial, the famous podcaster, better known as the Mindset Mentor, talks in one of the podcasts about the fallacy of "rewarding yourself"—feeling

---

79 Switchfoot, Vice Verses, 2011 – See Spotify Pay The Price Playlist for full lyrics and music.

that you've arrived, so it's time to take your foot off the pedal. It's not unlike when people reward themselves with a giant slice of carrot cake and a sugar-laced latte after a three-mile PB run... and in the process completely unravel all the benefits they acquired from the run.

So what is the Legacy Period?

I've tried to introduce the concept using the story of Anthony Lockwood, a lamplighter from Bolton in the 1940s.

Legacy is a strange word. It has so many definitions, and has been used in so many contexts, that it's almost lost its original meaning.

We think of someone who's died, or passed, and left some money or property in a will.

But the truth is legacy goes way beyond that. We are leaving a legacy every day, every moment, with every decision and contact that we make.

This thought struck me hard in the last three months.

Working as a pharmacist locum and consultant for a large pharmacy group, we took on a contract to join the national vaccination effort in the UK against flu and the coronavirus.

Over the course of the previous five years or so, and especially in 2020/21, I have personally vaccinated, or directly supervised the vaccination, of tens of thousands of people who have bravely and stoically travelled, sometimes hundreds of miles.

And my contact with every one of them has been literally one minute. But that one minute had the potential to change or save their lives.

Isn't that what legacy is about?

Leaving something of yourself that can change or support other people's lives?

For every customer who buys your product, uses your service, hears your podcast, reads your story on Instagram, listens to you speak, or meets you at a gig, you are leaving a little bit of your legacy.

Life is full of little legacies.

In this final part of the book, I want us to explore and unpack what it means to leave a legacy.

I argue that there are two categories of legacy an entrepreneur can leave behind: the Power Legacy and the Place Legacy.

The Power Legacy describes a situation in which the entrepreneur's legacy rests solely on his personal achievements apart from the company.

The Place Legacy describes a situation in which the entrepreneur is remembered primarily for what the company has achieved. In other words, she is remembered for what brought her fame in the first place.

From these two fundamental categories, we can discern four types:

- **The Philanthropist—Good Power, Bad Place:** The leader or entrepreneur has a good personal legacy, but a not-so good-business or organisational legacy. In other words, his legacy rests solely on his personal achievements.
- **The Purist—Good Place, Bad Power:** The leader or entrepreneur has a not-so-good or non-existent personal legacy but has succeeded in building a thriving and successful company or organisation. His legacy lies solely within the company he has built or the organisation he has founded or led.
- **The Profligate—Bad Power, Bad Place:** The entrepreneur or CEO has left a bad personal legacy and a failed business or organisational legacy.

- **The Pathfinder—Good Power, Good Place:** The legacy of the entrepreneur lies both with the organisation he founded or led and with his personal achievements outside the organisation.

Sometimes, principles and theories are best told through stories. So rather than explain what these types are with lengthy words and complicated charts, I will reveal what is most important about them through stories of four different people who epitomise these principles.

They've all left remarkable legacies, but in very different ways.

This can be summarised in the following table:

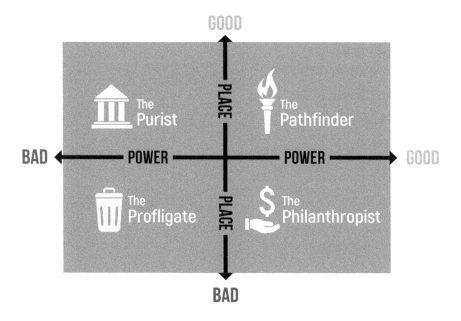

In the following chapters, we will explain in detail what these mean, the lessons they can teach us, and how to orient ourselves toward the ultimate legacy—that of the Pathfinder.

THE POWER LEGACY
THE PHILANTHROPIST—GOOD POWER, BAD PLACE

So, what is a Power Legacy?

The life that I have
Is all that I have
And the life that I have
Is yours.

The love that I have
Of the life that I have
Is yours and yours and yours.

…For the peace of my years
In the long green grass…
Will be yours and yours and yours.

- Leo Marks, "The Life That I Have"

I stumbled on this poem on a family trip in Wales in an old antique book. I was immediately drawn to it—the beauty in poetry is that you can fill in the gaps and make it yours.

Leo Marks was not a professional writer or poet. He was the head of the decoding offices of the Secret Service during the Second World War. During this time, a tragedy took place which gave birth to this poem.

Christmas Eve, 1943.

His girlfriend Ruth tragically died in a plane crash in Canada.

However, on 24 March, 1944, he dedicated it a second time to the French Secret agent Violette Szabo who was captured, tortured, and finally executed by the German army in 1945.

Oddly, there was a warmth in the words of this poem that resonated with the legacy of the Philanthropist—a life lived for the betterment of another.

The life I have is yours.

I felt a little story brewing in my mind as I stared out into the grass in my garden.

A date almost 25 years ago and, bizarrely, almost 49 years to the day the above poem was written.

23 March, 1998.

It was allegedly the largest gathering ever addressed by a sitting US president. No, it wasn't a Presidential inauguration on the lawn of the White House.

Nor was it a rallying cry during a war or a call to arms.

It was a political rally in a small country on the West Coast of Africa.

It was when President Bill Clinton visited Accra, Ghana and gave an address to over half a million Ghanaian people gathered just to hear him speak.

And to make the occasion even weirder, he shared the stage with a former military dictator who, two decades prior, had formed alliances with despots in countries such as Nicaragua, Cuba, and Zimbabwe and was involved in polarised Cold-War faceoffs with President Ronald Reagan.

President Jerry John Rawlings.

Years later, in 2004, Bill Clinton would reflect on the experience in his autobiography *My Life*, which sold over 2.3 million copies:

> My visit began in Ghana where President Jerry Rawlings and his wife got us to a rousing start in Independence Square; it was filled with more than half a million people…I liked Jerry Rawlings and respected the fact that after seizing power in a military coup, he was elected and re-elected president and was committed to relinquishing his office in 2000.[80]

Two years later, in a move that was almost unheard of in Africa, President Rawlings stepped down and handed over power to a democratically elected opposition government after almost two decades in power. He never made any attempt to rule through the back door, to regain power, or to intervene in any presidential election—he was given a number of roles by the UN and remained an internationally recognised diplomat, speaker, and envoy till his death in November 2020, which made headline news across the world.

How had this transformation happened? What was the primary factor for the transformation of a military dictator loathed by the West into a recognised, and some will argue celebrated, president of a middle-income country who had evolved to become a star pupil of the International Monetary Fund (IMF)?[81]

The seeds for this were sown almost 17 years earlier on June 16, 1982, when during a sleepless night in Plains, Georgia, another US President had an idea.

The principle of the Power Legacy, as I reiterated earlier, is that the entrepreneur is remembered mostly for a powerful life led **outside** what brought them to fame in the first place.

---

80 Clinton, William Jefferson. My Life (London, Random House, 2004) Pg 781.
81 https://www.imf.org/en/Countries/GHA/ghana-lending-case-study

Of the hundreds of people I thought about, nobody, in my opinion epitomises this more than President Jimmy Carter.

When President Richard Nixon resigned on August 9, 1974, after the infamous Watergate scandal, President Gerald Ford automatically assumed the presidency.

However, the disastrous presidency of Richard Nixon retained a dark shadow over his presidency, further complicated by his decision to issue an unconditional presidential pardon to his predecessor, the disastrous economic situation, persistent inflation, lingering anti-Republican sentiment, and a controversial and ineffectual televised presidential debate.

At the time, Jimmy Carter was a largely unknown figure from Georgia who held onto to strong Christian traditional values that people seemed to want after Nixon's corruption and Ford's guilt by association.

There was nothing about the early life of this unassuming young man to suggest he would later become the most powerful man in the world.

His civilian life after a stint in the Navy was unassuming. He lived in public housing in Plains, Georgia, then was forced to become an agribusiness entrepreneur after his father, James Carter, a peanut farmer who, after having created a successful peanut farm, contracted a severe form of pancreatic cancer and was given weeks to live.

His family was having a hard time coping with the grief and the business, and Carter, being the first son who had been away from the family on naval duty, felt responsible.

It was then that he made a dramatic decision that was to completely alter the trajectory of his life.

He resigned from the navy.

This caused a major rift between him and Rosalynn, but he stuck to his guns and decided to relocate to Plains, Georgia to spend the last weeks of his dad's life with him, take care of his mother, and look after the farm.

His dad passed away soon after, and Jimmy was left with the arduous task of managing his dad's estate despite having no prior significant experience of entrepreneurship, management, or peanut farming.

However, Carter took up classes in business and read up on agriculture, whilst his wife, Rosalynn, learned accounting to manage the business's books. Life was tough. The first year's harvest failed, largely due to drought. Carter had to borrow a lot of money through various lines of credit to keep the business solvent—it barely broke even in its first year.

Nevertheless, they stuck with it, grew the business, and became quite successful—tending thousands of acres of land and building warehouses to store over 15,000 tons of peanuts, as well as storage facilities for cotton, corn, and small grains.

Producing seed peanuts evolved into a major source of income, and Carter was soon contracting with other farmers to produce seed on their land for him to process in his own personally designed shelling plant.

He founded Carter's Warehouse, which became a one-stop shop for everything needed for local farmers. This became a major family operation which evolved and lasted for over 23 years and which only ended when he was elected president.

In his autobiography, *A Full Life—Reflections at 90*, he summarised it this way:

> I became reasonably proficient in farming, forestry, business management and leadership in state-wide organisations related to these duties. I also tried to master as many skills as possible, including construction with wood, steel, and concrete, and the maintenance of our equipment.

> It was hard work, twelve months a year, but I enjoyed the challenges, and our
> multiple businesses prospered. I became deeply interested in environmental issues
> by meeting challenges on our own land and working with others.[82]

But being a restless soul, he felt the pull to enter politics, not the least
by the perceived injustices he saw in racism, poverty, and the disastrous
Watergate scandal. After a controversial election, he won the Georgia State
Senate seat, where he served for two terms.

His stand against segregation lost him the first election in which he ran
for Georgia governor, but he stood again for the next term and won. This
catapulted him to the national stage where, after a particularly fractious
election, he became president.

Jimmy Carter did not prove to be a popular president. There's that age-old
cliché that his presidency was largely a failure, but he's the best ex-president
the country has ever had.

He was perceived as difficult to work with, stubbornly independent and
ineffectual at building coalitions, and indecisive and incapable of running
the country.

This perceived "failure" was greatly exacerbated by the seizure of the US
embassy in Tehran and the subsequent holding hostage of 52 Americans
at the end of his presidency.

By July 1980, his popularity had irreversibly tanked. He had the lowest
polling approval of any US president since polls were recorded, with his
approval rating at 21 percent.

Ronald Reagan won the election by an enormous landslide, taking 489
electoral votes compared to Jimmy Carter's 49, the biggest victory by a
non-incumbent in the history of the United States.

---

82 Carter, Jimmy. A Full Life- Reflections at Ninety (New York, Simon & Schuster 2015)

Unlike Jimmy Carter, Ronald Reagan proved to be a very effective, popular, and decisive president and is still revered today by the Republican Party in particular and by the United States as a whole.

It seemed that like Richard Nixon, and Gerald Ford before him, the legacy of Jimmy Carter was doomed to the ignominious dark side of the history books.

How wrong that was.

At 56 years old, Jimmy Carter was one of the youngest ex-presidents. He and Rosalynn retired, with no idea what to do next.

But one night in 1981 after only a few hours of sleep, he called Rosalynn and made another decision which completely changed the trajectory of his life and propelled him toward the role of what biographer Jonathan Alter calls "a world-class humanitarian who set a new standard for former new presidents."

In his exact words, Carter said:

> I know what we can do for the future. We can create a place near our presidential library and museum and invite people to come there like Anwar Sadat and Menachem Begin came to Camp David. I can offer my services as a mediator to help prevent or resolve conflicts either within or between nations. If they prefer, I can go to their country.[83]

By these words, the Carter Center was born and was established legally in 1982.

The Carter Center adopted a few basic principles:

• It would be nonpartisan

---

83 Ibid, Pg 208

- It would be as innovative as possible, not duplicating or competing with other organisations that were addressing issues successfully
- It would always operate on a balanced budget
- It would not be afraid of possible failure if the goals were worthwhile

President Carter expanded the concept of The Carter Center by including conferences of important issues in which he had been involved as president—peace in the Middle East, international security and arms control, business and the environment, education, and global health.

The Carter Center now has a budget of $100 million annually, with another $100 million in contributions of medicines and other supplies that are distributed in countries throughout Africa and Latin America.

It boasts a staff of 180 full-time people, supplemented by several hundred trained experts and thousands of unpaid volunteers who have been trained to work on projects in targeted countries.

It is now active in 80 countries, promoting peace, human rights, democracy and freedom and better healthcare.

The Carter Center has chalked some incredible achievements:

- Treating 35 million worldwide for malaria and the five neglected diseases— onchocerciasis, schistosomiasis, elephantiasis, trachoma, and guinea worm.
- Organizing Global 2000 in partnership with Nobel laureate Norman Borlaug and philanthropist Ryoichi Sasakawa, an agricultural programme designed to increase production of food grains in several countries in Africa including Ghana, Sudan, Zambia, and Zimbabwe, and to teach 8 million families how to double their output of maize, wheat, corn, rice, and sorghum.
- Resolving a crisis in 1994 that would almost certainly have resulted in war in Haiti when the elected leader, Jean-Bertrand Arisitide, had

been forced into exile and President Bill Clinton had sent planes to invade Haiti.

- Monitoring the parliamentary and presidential elections in Egypt from 2010 to 2012 following the overthrow of President Mubarak.
- Monitoring over 100 elections throughout the world, the 99th being the Tunisian presidential election in December 2014. Three or four of these are done every year.
- Completing houses in partnership with Habitat for Humanity in many American states and in Hungary, South Africa, Mexico, South Korea, Canada, the Philippines, Haiti, China, Vietnam, Laos, Thailand, Cambodia, South Korea, and Nepal.

It was the Carter Center's declaration of the free and fair results in the 1992 Ghana democratic election that paved the way for President Jerry Rawlings to make the switch from a military dictator to a bona fide internationally recognised, democratically elected president, which in turn brought Ghana from the brink of being a pariah state to a beacon of African democracy, relative prosperity, and business today.

And unlike President Obama's controversial 2009 Nobel Peace Prize, there was not one single voice of dissent when Jimmy Carter was awarded that prize in 2002.

His legacy will always be that of the Philanthropist. Good Power, bad Place.

So to paraphrase Leo Marks's poem,

...For the peace of His years
In the long green grass...
Will be ours and ours and ours...

Where he had "failed" as a president, he had more than made amends for it in his private life, the direct opposite of our next legacy type: the Purist.

THE PLACE LEGACY
THE PURIST—GOOD PLACE, BAD POWER

You remember sometimes
That the place is by the sea
And once in a while you see a gull
Rise
Swift against the blazing sun
In dazzling shards of a noonday
It's always so swift, so brief
At night you recall it all
While the door is locked.

- - Kofi Awoonor, "The Place," *The Promise of Hope*, 2014

There is a picture which haunts me every time I look at my phone, type on my Mac, and find myself considering the genius of those products. That picture is engraved into my psyche.

It just reminds me of the brevity—and associated paradoxes of life—and as one of my favourite authors, Ben Horowitz, says in his characteristic blunt style in his 2019 book *What You Do Is Who You Are,* "Keep death in mind at all times, like a samurai—it's good for business."

It's a picture of the former Apple CEO Steve Jobs.

It's a haunting picture of his last days, when he was riddled with cancer. He stands, extremely scrawny, in a black pullover and shorts, with oddly coloured socks and geriatric sandals that I usually associate with the 80 and 90-year-old men who trudge past me in the city centre with their black Zimmer frames.

He stands with a faint appearance of resigned acceptance on his face, looking absentmindedly into the distance. He looks so gaunt and frail that it is almost impossible to reconcile him with the man who rejuvenated Apple less than a decade beforehand.

But yes, he was one and the same man. No doubt.

Volumes of countless reams have been written about this man. I wondered long and hard as to whether the world was ready to read yet another thesis about his legacy.

Yet try as I might, there was no better man on this planet to exemplify this type of legacy.

Of the numerous articles, books, movies, and documentaries that have explored the life of Steven Jobs, one of my favourites is from the 2012 Harvard Business Review—"The Real Leadership Lessons of Steve Jobs" by Walter Isaacson.

The 15 lessons Isaacson enumerates in the article provide insight into the legacy that Jobs left behind which focused on the ruthless focus of Steve Jobs on creating beautiful Apple products.[84]

Simon Sinek arrives at a similar premise:

> Start with why. *Everything we do is about challenging the status quo. We believe in thinking differently, and we prove this by making beautiful, user-friendly products. Oh, and we happened to make great computers. Wanna buy one?*[85]

He was consumed by the products that Apple made and nothing else. Everything else—the environment, the staff, the people, everything, even his own life—took a backseat and was sacrificed at the altar of making Apple products the best they could be.

---

84 https://hbr.org/2012/04/the-real-leadership-lessons-of-steve-jobs
85 Sinek, Simon. Start with why – How Great Leaders Inspire Everyone to take Action (London, Penguin 2011)

Undoubtedly, that has yielded fascinating results.

Take the iPhone, for instance.

It is the single most successful product of all time. Apple has sold more than 1.2 billion iPhones in the 10 years since the first one was introduced, and cumulative sales are closing in on $1 trillion. Apple's profits per phone are 30-40 percent profit margins, and even now, its market share continues to grow.

Contrast this with Samsung, whose profit margins per phone are rumoured to be around 17 percent.

Steve Jobs made Apple great not only by designing great and beautiful products, but by connecting its pitches to its product design efforts—the idea that everything Apple does is about challenging the status quo, doing things differently, and connecting its products to its consumer—through iCloud, end-to-end control, and a seamless user experience.

Yes, and most customers agree.

I'm hooked on Apple, despite the persistent and disapproving comments from my teenage son, who plans to study software engineering, and my brother, who is a computer security and software guru and can surely claim to know better.

The legacy of Steve Jobs typifies the legacy of the Purist.

I introduced the concept of the Purist in my introduction to the Legacy Period earlier.

The traditional definition of a purist from the Merriam-Webster Dictionary is the following:

*"A person who adheres strictly and often excessively to a tradition—especially one preoccupied with the purity of a language and its **protection from the use of foreign and altered forms.** "*[86]

I have adapted this definition for the purposes of the Legacy Period as the following:

A Purist is one who is solely remembered uniquely and exclusively for the organisation, company, or movement he founded, formed, or led.

Steve Jobs is the ironclad definition of a Purist.

A man who will almost exclusively be remembered for the work he did at Apple.

No more, no less.

A man whose legacy is inseparable from the legacy of the world's first trillion-dollar company.

No more, no less.

Steve Jobs is (now was) Apple, and Apple was Steve Jobs.

I firmly believe that Steve Jobs's best decision was not the iPhone, beautifying the Mac, or inventing the iPad.

It is a decision he is given the least credit for.

It is in choosing Tim Cook to be his successor.

Steve Jobs built one of the most successful companies in the world.

---

86 Merriam-Webster definition of a Purist (noun) https://www.merriam-webster.com/dictionary/purist

But Tim Cook may well be building one of the most successful, **enduring, and lasting** companies in the world.

Out of interest, I did a snap poll, completely unscientific, to see how well people knew Tim Cook. Even after a decade, everyone knew Steve Jobs. Without exception. I was shocked that after a decade at the helm, over 80 percent of the 20 or so people I asked still knew little or nothing of Tim Cook.

In his book *Enduring Success: What We Can Learn from the History of Outstanding Corporations*, bestselling author and professor Christian Stadler says that for a company to enjoy enduring success, its strategy, organisation, and environment need to be in strategic alignment all the time. This is a dynamic process, which he illustrates in his HOW framework for enduring success (see below).

He puts it this way:

> The challenge for corporations is no different than the challenge a society faces. Companies must find ways of operating in harmony with their environment. They need to match their resources and capabilities with their environmental opportunities. As the business environment is constantly changing, companies must modify their strategies and organisations. If they fail to do so over an extended period of time…they will cease to exist.

He continues (refer to the picture on the following page):

> In Stage 1, a company's capabilities are aligned with the environment in which it operates. At some point (Stage II) the environment will change, and the company will no longer achieve a strategic fit. Whether the firm will succeed in the long run depends on its ability to change its strategy and organisation to once again achieve this alignment (Stage III).

From his research into the principles behind centuries-old European companies that are still thriving, he points to five strategies that underlie enduring success:

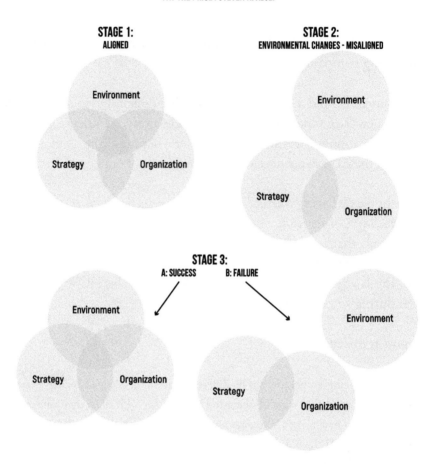

1. Companies need to put exploitation first and exploration second.
2. Companies need to act conservatively with their finances.
3. Companies need to develop mechanisms that allow them to learn over time and space.
4. Companies need to diversify into related businesses.
5. Companies need to manage change in a culturally sensitive way.[87]

Going into details on what makes successful companies endure is outside the scope of this book, (A list of recommended books are provided at the end of this which explore this further), and whilst *Enduring Success* by

---

87 Stadler, Christian, Enduring Success; What we can learn from the History of Outstanding Corporations (California, Stanford University Press, 2011)

Christian Stadler and *Built to Last* and *Beyond Entrepreneurship* by Jim Collins come to slightly different conclusions, they have all emphasis on one thing—companies that last continually produce good leaders, products, and services over extended periods of time.

However, I contend that Steve Jobs's relentless focus on products over everything else meant that over time, Apple was likely to get out of sync with the environment in which it was operating if it didn't make decisions that would ensure it remained in sync with its environment.

It's striking that many business books at the time looked exclusively at Apple's market share and results as an excuse to justify Steve Jobs's approach to leadership and management.

But the environment is shifting toward what Chris Lewis and Pippa Malmgren call the concept of the infinite leader:

> *Business is still about people—people operate across paradoxes and opposing forces, in a world that confounds these influences. Leaders need to continuously juggle and neutralize these to succeed. Be what your people need you to be and learn what they don't teach you in business schools; remain analytical and numbers-focused when needed, but also bring your heart, person, and integrity to leadership.[88]*

With this in mind, I want to highlight five things that Tim Cook brought to Apple and that Steve Jobs ignored or dismissed. Leander Kahney's brilliant new book *Tim Cook: The Genius Who Took Apple to the Next Level* (2019, Penguin Business) lists many of his achievements in direct contrast to Steve Jobs, which I have paraphrased below:

- *Philanthropic Efforts:* Steve Jobs was extremely stingy when it came to philanthropy. He argued that the best thing he could do for charity was to increase its value, so shareholders amassed more income

---

88 Lewis & Malmgren *The Infinite Leader: Balancing the Demands of Modern Business Leadership* (London, Kogan Page, 2021)

to give away to charitable causes of their choices. He differed like chalk and cheese with Steven Wozniak, his cofounder, in this regard. Apple made no significant donations to charity under Jobs (with the PRODUCT RED) collaboration with U2 frontman Bono being a notable exception), and neither did Jobs himself donate any great proportion of his estimated $10 billion when he died. Tim Cook completely reversed this trend when he took over. Within five months of becoming Apple's CEO, he announced that he would donate his entire fortune to charitable causes and as CEO has instituted a new charitable matching program for employees where Apple will match donations of up to $10 thousand per employee per year. Just two months after this announcement, Apple had donated over $2 million. Apple has also donated hundreds of millions of dollars since 2011 to various educational, environmental, healthcare, and human rights. To make this even more remarkable, Tim Cook made this decision during a particularly tumultuous first year as CEO of Apple.

- *Commitment to the Environment:* Apple is now considered one of the greenest companies in its field, and this only happened after Tim Cook had taken over as CEO. The almost near-paranoid commitment to perfection and product design by Jobs was exemplified when he refused to allow sustainability organisations to stamp recycling codes onto products that weighed more than 25 grams because the codes "were not pretty." Kahner quotes a senior manager from Apple who said on anonymity that for Steve Jobs, "Pure looks trumped any responsible consideration for sustainability." A 2011 report on environmental practices by large companies in China ranked Apple at the bottom, and it was reported that Chinese workers had been hospitalised after exposure to a chemical that was used to clean iPhone screens. Apple was also labelled as the least-green tech company in a 2011 report on the environmental impact of cloud computing. It also received the lowest percentage on the "Clean Energy Index" by Greenpeace. Greenpeace and other activists started to protest outside Apple's headquarters, acts which went ignored by Jobs. When Tim Cook took over, he acted fast to clean up this mess—recruiting the former head of the EPA, switching to more renewable energy sources, ramping up partnerships with solar companies, and personally investing his time and energy into reversing this trend.

- *Encouraging Diversity:* Steve Jobs's senior leadership team was overwhelmingly white and male, and he paid little attention to issues of diversity with regard to sexuality, gender, or race. Even though this is still an issue at Apple, Cook has been more proactive about hiring women and people of colour to executive positions. For instance, Lisa Jackson, who was the first black woman to head the EPA, was in charge of Apple's environmental issues in 2013. Denise Young in 2014 was the head of human resources and later on became head of diversity and inclusion. Latino Eddy Cue is now SVP of Internet software and services, Angela Ahrendts, former CEO of Burberry, oversaw Apple's retail stores—and crucially, people of colour play a larger role in advertising campaigns, managing retail stores, and bringing more diversity to Apple products. Even though more work needs to be done here, Tim Cook is clearly on the right track.

- *Commitment to Privacy in an Increasingly Open World:* One of Tim Cook's markedly different approaches is his relentless quest for data privacy. No doubt this is partly borne out of his own desire to stay out of the limelight as much as possible. "Apple doesn't want your data" is his continual mantra. In an era where all our sensitive information is available, it is mind-boggling to think what Apple could do if they could mine this data and sell it to advertisers. He has championed encryption and explained why Apple refused to provide a backdoor to allow governments to hack into IOS devices—a stand which brought much controversy, especially in the light of terrorism. He paid a heavy price for this, but ultimately came out a winner as public opinion shifted.

- *Looking After Workers Who Supplied Components for Apple Products:* After having outsourced Apple's products to FoxConn and to China, public scrutiny was inevitably going to fall on how these overseas factories treated their staff. Tim Cook has led efforts to make sure that overseas employees who work to produce Apple products are treated fairly, are not exploited, and are paid fairly for what they do. This is one area where Steve Jobs never took notice and was criticised continually.

In taking these five major steps, Tim Cook has reversed Steve Jobs's ambivalence regarding issues outside his laser focus for product quality and hopefully realigned the stars in favour of Apple becoming an enduring company and not going the way of BlackBerry and Nokia before it.

So what does this teach us?

The premise of success I defined at the earlier part of this book. Success cannot just be based on financial performance. If there is one thing we have learned from Tim Cook, it is that. And that is what Steve Jobs failed to grasp, but Tim Cook knew instinctively.

But for Steve Jobs, his legacy will always be the legacy of the Purist—his unwavering commitment and focus to designing beautiful products for Apple and making Apple the number-one tech company in the world, excluding everything else.

In his book *What You Do Is What You Are*, author Ben Horowitz calls Steve Jobs a wartime CEO and Tim Cook a peacetime CEO. He claims a wartime CEO has to place victory ahead of protocol on occasion, and a calmer peacetime CEO focuses more on good protocol and longer-term success. He claims that switching between both is very hard and may need different management teams.[89]

I fundamentally disagree with this assessment. Tim Cook has fought just as hard for Apple as Steve Jobs has. The big difference, as I have pointed out, is that Tim Cook is more of what Pippa Malmgren and Chris Lewis have called the infinite leader—he has better balanced the demands of modern business leadership by focusing on the wider picture and the wider ethical world, and that there is a world out there beyond just beautiful Apple products.

But there is another kind of legacy. One full of Red Flag Pains and waste. And it's to that legacy, the Profligate, that we turn to next.

---

89 Horowitz, Ben. What You Do is Who You Are: How to Create Your Business Culture (New York HarperCollins, 2019)

THE PASSOVER LEGACIES
THE PROFLIGATE—BAD POWER, BAD PLACE

Oh who is that young sinner with the handcuffs on his wrists?
And what has he been after that they groan and shake their fists?
And wherefore is he wearing such a conscience-stricken air?
Oh they're taking him to prison for the colour of his hair.

'Tis a shame to human nature, such a head of hair as his;
In the good old time 'twas hanging for the colour that it is;
Though hanging isn't bad enough and flaying would be fair
For the nameless and abominable colour of his hair

Oh a deal of pains he's taken and a pretty price he's paid
To hide his poll or dye it of a mentionable shade;
But they've pulled the beggar's hat off for the world to see and stare;
And they're holding him to justice for the colour of his hair

...And between the spells of labour in the time he has to spare
He can curse the God that made him for the colour of his hair.

- A.E. Houseman, "Oh Who Is That Young Sinner"

This is a brilliant poem.

But what many people didn't realise at the time was that it was inspired by a real incident, when the famous poet and celebrity personality Oscar Wilde was briefly at Clapham Junction Train Station in London, being transferred to Reading Gaol on charges of sexual offences.

He was recognised by the mob and spat at, and Housman writes from the position of an observer.

Oscar Wilde was flamboyant, classy, witty, and one of the best-known personalities of his day. Although it was widely believed that the charges were related to Wilde's consensual homosexual activities, recent research suggests that he was also a paedophile, who used his charisma, fame, riches, and personality to take advantage of young teenagers.[90]

And although there are stark differences from Oscar Wilde, this poem did remind me of a similar person, a famously flamboyant, extremely talented, charismatic, and rich personality who used his fame and riches to take advantage of little underage girls and in so doing brought disgrace and ignominy which rattled all the way from the United States presidency and the financial institutions of the United States, across the pond and right down to the Royal Family.

Jeffrey Edward Epstein (1953- 2019).

The legacy of Jeffrey Edward Epstein is the legacy of the Profligate.

A wasted, wasted life on every count.

The nameless and shameless abominable colour of his hair.

What can I say? I just like young girls.[91]

Jeffrey Epstein.

And yet, things could have been so very different.

In *The Spider*, author Barry Levine traces Jeffrey Epstein's life.[92] His parents, Seymour and Pauline Epstein, insisted their boys did well in school and enrolled them in P.S. 188, a ten-minute walk from home. He was aptly

---

90 https://www.huffpost.com/entry/why-are-these-artists-def_b_372
91 https://nypost.com/2020/07/11/jeffrey-epsteins-first-victim-was-17-year-old-from-london-book-claims/
92 Levine, Barry. The Spider (New York, Crown Random House, 2020) – This book was the main source for this section.

nicknamed Bear. He loved maths and science, liked music, and played the piano. But he was classified as being so gifted and talented that he was promoted and skipped third grade—a process which was repeated in the seventh grade. In fact, he was so talented that he walked out of high school with a diploma at only sixteen years of age.

He continued to Cooper Union, a university in Lower Manhattan known for producing some of the best architects and engineers in the United States. It offered full scholarships to all its undergraduates and was one of the most selective schools in the country, accepting less than 13 percent of all its applicants. But he didn't finish and dropped out. He re-enrolled in New York University's elite Courant Institute of Mathematical Sciences, where, again, he dropped out after three years without completing his degree.

He was bent on chartering his own course—his own way.

The year was 1974.

And from here, the deception began.

It started with his getting hired at Dalton School on Manhattan's Upper East Side. It is consistently ranked as one of America's top preparatory and prestigious academies. How a 21-year-old with no degree got hired is still a mystery. The school boasted that 75 percent of its staff had advanced degrees, and the remaining 25 percent had completed their undergraduate degrees. Apart from one.

He was unconventional in every sense—wore gold chains and dressed flamboyantly, spoke with an odd, working-class accent, and began to sow the seeds which would become his one of his two Red Flag Pains, an inexplicable attraction to underage girls.

Then, in 1975, he inexplicably left Dalton.

Well, not quite inexplicably. The official line was that he "had not grown as a new teacher to the standard of the school."

But as author Barry Levine dug deeper, he uncovered the reason.

At a parent-teacher conference at the school, Epstein was introduced to the CEO of Bear Stearns, Alan Greenberg, who was the father of one of the students, Lynne. Alan, who was a "rags to riches" sort of CEO, saw himself in Epstein. Epstein reportedly confided in the CEO that he didn't want to be a teacher anymore. Greenberg summoned him to his office, "barked out a few questions," and hired him on the spot.

At Bear Stearns, he could do no wrong. His talent and academic brilliance shone through, and he was able to apply his scientific background to his trades. He was renowned for his ability to comprehend the world of options, and his approached reaped instant and lucrative dividends.

Greenberg loved him and showed him off to his associates and friends, and within just two to three years, he had a web of wealthy and exclusive clients. He was now earning ten times more than he'd been earning at Dalton.

But his second Red Flag Pain which started at Dalton was conceived, nurtured, and hatched here.

Deceit.

It came out that he had lied on his résumé. Issues with his expense accounts. Insider trading irregularities. These resulted in his losing his licenses.

In 1981, faced with little choice, he cleared his desk and collected a $100,000 bonus.

And in the same year, he became an entrepreneur, founding his own consulting firm, Intercontinental Assets Group Inc (IAG), which was formed to "assist clients in recovering stolen money from fraudulent brokers and lawyers."

But the name ring was hollow. There were no other staff members or employees. There was no receptionist. No clients. Company files were just stacked on any available space in the posh flat. But the name did have one thing: ambition.

Epstein had it in spades.

And that ambition began to become reality when he was introduced to Hoffenberg in 1987 by one of his clients at IAG. Hoffenberg, a fellow Brooklyn native, ran Towers Financial Corporation, a firm that purchased bad debt and then turned it into considerable profit. The two hit it off, and Epstein was adored by Hoffenberg.

Unsurprisingly, he became a consultant for Hoffenberg's Towers Financial soon after, earning $25,000 a month and, according to Levine, grew the company's revenue-raising division from an annual turnover of $20 million to just under $1 billion.

Towers Financial attempted to take over Pan Am and Emery Air Freight, both of which failed, depleted the insurance firms of their assets, and cost thousands of investors over $450 million.

However, they started again, trying to recover their losses with fraud, using a promissory note Ponzi scheme that promised 20 percent returns. They amassed a great deal of wealth which they both siphoned off. The enormity of the scheme caught the attention of US attorneys in Illinois and New York.

Hoffenberg ended up doing 18 years in prison, and Epstein, almost miraculously, escaped without a smear.

He was now rich.

In 1990, aged 37, Jeffrey Edward Epstein purchased a two-story mansion at 358 El Brillo Way in Palm Beach, Florida, one of the most exclusive areas of one of the richest suburbs in Florida.

He now shared a street with one Donald Trump.

It was here, at this address, that the abuses took on a life of their own.

It was here that hundreds of underage girls were abused, raped, and irreparably damaged for life.

And how he got away with it for so long still is somewhat of a mystery.

But when he went down, he brought a lot of people down with him. Prince Andrew, Barclays CEO Jes Staley, former CEO of private equity firm Apollo Global Management, Leon Black.

This is to say nothing of the long list of celebrities who were forced to defend their reputations. Donald Trump, Bill Clinton, Joi Ito, Bill Gates, Glenn Dubin, and US attorney Alex Acosta. It even stretched as far as Shimon Peres and Ehud Barak, Israel's former PMs.

Epstein made sure he had control in two ways: his black book, which contained addresses and contact details for politicians, business leaders, and decision-makers across the whole world, and a world-class surveillance system in every room on all his properties, where incriminating acts of both his closest friends and were printed, filmed, secured and safeguarded.

They all "owed him favours," as he put it.

Not to mention his co-conspirator, Ghislane Maxwell.

Very possibly due to this control, he was able to drive through a great many red flags before his sins finally caught up with him.

The things he did were really sickening. And it had become so ingrained in his psyche that even on 24 September, 2007, when the blueprint of a deal between the US government and Jeffrey Epstein was negotiated, the abuse continued with girls as young as 14.

In reading the book and researching for this book, one thing that remained in my mind were the words of a victim who said, "I spent two weeks vomiting almost to death in a hospital after the first encounter."

He applied for work release while imprisoned, under strict conditions, and even when he was at work during the day, the abuse continued for the 13 months he served in custody.

That is the problem with Red Flag Pain hits. The phantom fixes they offer are never enough, and you need more and more and more to get the same hit.

But weirdly, one thing was always on his mind, which he talked about constantly.

His legacy.

In an interview with a publicist in 2016, he said, "I don't want billionaire pervert to be the first line of my obituary."

As he approached 50, it began to dawn upon him that he was destined to be unmarried. He wanted a child through Virginia Roberts, a girl who he had abused for years and had now become his arranger in chief for young girls. He offered her a mansion and stipend for life if she would bear him a child and sign away the rights. This riled Virginia to no end and was a catalyst for her to finally leave for good. She eventually got married to an Australian martial artist named Robert Giuffre and took his last name. A biological legacy was out of the question.

So how about a Power Legacy?

Well, he was fascinated with science and held many conferences on scientific subjects on his private island in Little Saint James. For example, he convened a meeting of artificial intelligence experts organised by his good friend and top scientist Marvin Minsky in 2002 and another one for 21 top physicists for a conference on gravity in 2006 which included

Stephen Hawking, where there were always young girls in tow. He also hosted lunches at Harvard University's Program for Evolutionary Dynamics (PED) which he had helped launch with a $6.5 million donation. The PED had ambitions to "study the fundamental mathematical principles that guide evolution, including the evolution of cancer, viruses, and economics, and to rid the world of cancer."

According to Slate, he told a long-time friend, "I only have two interests in life, science, and p@£$%%y." As the scientists were holding their discussions in a small room, Epstein was in the back, on a couch, hugging and kissing these girls.[93]

His acquaintances were like a who's who of top world scientists: bestselling author Stephen Hawking; palaeontologist and evolutionary scientist Stephen Jay Gould; Oliver Sacks; neurologist George Sacks; George Church; Nobel laureate Murray Gell-Mann; and physicist Frank Wilczek.

At some point, he was donating up to $20 million per year to scientific causes affiliated with MIT, Harvard, and numerous other charities and organisations. He wanted to be known as a "science philanthropist."

It was clearly a passion of his and where he obviously wanted to leave his legacy, even though his ideas bordered on the bizarre and pure lunacy, such as describing a plan to inseminate women in his ranch in New Mexico or impregnate 20 women at a time as a means of "strengthening his gene pool."

Clearly, his Red Flag Pain had infected what could have and would have been genuine legacy goals for any businessman or philanthropist.

In the end, all the charities he supported, all the causes to which he gave, all the dinners he hosted—it all came to nothing. Celebrities lined up to

---

93 https://www.google.com/url?client=internal-element-cse&cx=011089738672311785372:yrshx-u5c-pw&q=https://slate.com/technology/2019/08/jeffrey-epstein-science-eugenics-sexual-abuse-researchers.html&sa=U&ved=2ahUKEwickLCOhf73AhXXu6QKHbyVAP8QFnoECAcQAg&usg=AOvVaw3Vaz-ciVeHdGeqfwq337_ZC

discredit him, disown him, and distance themselves from him. Charities lined up to return the money and denounce him.

His life was wasted—all those gifts, the charisma, the kindness (and yes, he was kind according to all that knew him), the intelligence, and the charm were wasted because he refused to stop at the red traffic lights from his Dalton days.

He became a failure. Personally, professionally, and ethically.

That red flag finally brought him to his knees in the end. Literally.

He was found hanging by apparent suicide, when he was discovered in his cell on Saturday, 10 August, 2019 after he had been arrested again.

And yet...

As I read his biography, and researched his life for this book, it forced me to confront my own Red Flag Pain I had battled for decades.

The what-ifs filled my mind.

What if I hadn't reached out to my vicar and best friend Paul Wright and Geoff Lee that cold morning in June 2016?

What if I hadn't reached out to Covenant Eyes to help me stop watching pornography?

What if I didn't have a loving and supportive wife who stood by me and believed in me and gave me a second chance?

What if I didn't have a tight circle of friends and family who stood by me and didn't judge me and treat me like an outcast?

What if? What if? What if?

I could easily have gone the same way.

Nobody is born a monster. Or maybe everybody is born a monster. Our responses to our vices will determine our verses, our stories, yes, even our legacies.

And as if from nowhere, a poem began to form in my morning reflection. My reflections on Red Flag Pain began to surface. And the tears, again, began to flow. I grabbed my journal and pen:

How different things could have been...

As I looked down
The snake bared its fangs
And I turned away
Horrified.

But the palm wine
Had already been poured
And the fat genie
Had already left the bottle.

A Passion unleashed
But as the Tears flowed freely
I came to my senses
As the Penny dropped.

What's mine is mine
And what's yours is yours
And ne'er the Twain
Shall meet.

- Steven N. Adjei, "#Engulfed"

And I made a daily commitment to myself and to my destiny, my future self. Never again will I allow my Red Flag Pain to destroy my legacy.

What's mine (my future) is mine, and what's his (my past) is his, and never the twain shall meet.

I made a commitment to never let my legacy be that of the Profligate.

And as you, dear reader, turn away horrified, I hope that the Profligate Legacy of Jeffrey Edward Epstein will force you to reflect and to banish every inch of Red Flag Pain.

Why?

Because there is a better way. A more excellent way. A way to decide to end, even before you begin.

A way to leave a good Power Legacy **AND** a good Place Legacy.

It is the legacy of the Pathfinder.

And it is to this legacy that we now turn.

THE PATHFINDER—GOOD POWER, GOOD PLACE

Eventually they're gonna know who's right
To make a stand, you've got to win the fight
Can't stand the heat then just stay out the light
For you might never make it out alive
You gotta live without a compromise
Let everybody hear your battle cry

Yeah, we're gonna be legends
Gonna get their attention
What we're doing here ain't just scary
It's about to be legendary
Yeah, we're gonna be legends
Gonna teach 'em all a lesson
Got this feeling in our souls we carry
It's about to be legendary

- Welshly Arms, "Legendary," *Legendary*, 2019

"One that goes ahead and discovers or shows others a path or a way"
- The Oxford English Dictionary

It is a week before Christmas, December, 2018. Cassarina has lung cancer.[94] She is 69 years old. Her gaunt frame, tired-looking eyes, and limping frame give an indication of the pain she is suffering inside. She is on

---

94 Zimbabwe's Hospitals turn sick patients away as strike continues: https://www.youtube.com/watch?v=P-dc6x5nkHZY accessed 10 Feb 2022.

chemotherapy. It's been helping, and it has been subsidised by the state, making the medication affordable.

Every morning, her lung discharges a smelly fluid which has to be cleaned by her daughter, Margaret—and she was given some cheap painkillers to alleviate the pain.

But she's looking forward to that day, 19 December, 2019, when that lung will finally be removed.

She trudges along to the country's biggest hospital in the capital with her daughter that morning, full of hope—to get her second round of medicines. As she gets out of the taxi, she is greeted by a huge crowd with placards, demonstrating in front of the hospital. They were on their way, marching to Parliament. She recognises two of her cancer nurses and the doctor in the crowd.

There is shouting. Cars tooting their horns. The sun seemed hotter. The hospital cancer ward seemed strangely empty of patients.

But the pain is unbearable. She has just one goal: to get to the hospital to see her consultant, get a few tests done to ascertain the state of the growth in her lung, and get a prescription filled for some more medication, after the operation to remove her lung.

But it isn't to be.

She is turned away at the door and asked to go to a private pharmacy for a repeat on her medication.

She is confused. But she obliges.

She gets to the pharmacy across the road. Hands in her old prescription. The bill comes, quoted in US dollars.

But Cassarina does not live in the US. She lives in Zimbabwe, a land-locked country in Southern Africa. Inflation is running at 500 percent. Prices are increasing up to tenfold **daily.** The country issued a banknote of a HUNDRED TRILLION Zimbabwean dollars at some point. So the local money is essentially worthless. To add insult to injury, the family had already paid $400 towards her treatment up to this point.

With no chance of the operation happening that day, she returns home. The pain is even worse, bordering on unbearable by this point.

Miracle (not her real name) had lost three relatives during the strike: her mother-in-law, uncle, and now cousin.

A pregnant woman, Endeavour, had a huge gash above her eye where she had been beaten by her husband and could not feel her baby moving. She had been turned away from Parirenyatwa and was trying Harare Main Hospital.

No luck.

Zimbabwe's busiest hospital, Parirenyatwa Hospital, in November 2019 was like a ghost park.

Almost all Zimbabwe's 3500 doctors, as well as pharmacists, nurses, and auxiliary workers, were on strike. With most doctors earning less than $100 a month, whilst nurses were on half that, who could blame them? The salary was gobbled up by transport and food alone. And to make things worse, basic supplies needed for them to perform their duties were in shortage—senior doctors described the hospitals, paradoxically, as "death traps."

The country's already-teetering healthcare system had come to a screeching halt.

The government was in a bind. It tried to act tough by firing the doctors. 448 had lost their jobs, and another 150 faced being dragged into disciplinary hearings. When this backfired, they allegedly started bringing

Army physicians and importing much-needed supplies. This also backfired. The union leader, Dr. Peter Magombeyi, had already been abducted mysteriously for almost a week.

But again, the hypocrisy of the politicians were brought to the fore. The then Vice President, Constantino Chiwenga, had just returned from being treated for an undisclosed illness in South Africa and China on a private chartered Chinese plane where he had been away for four months. He was one of the loudest critics of the doctors.

But patients continued to die or get turned away, and the standoff continued. A month. Two months. Two months and three weeks.

Each position was hardening, and people continued to suffer.

Until a resolution came. On 21 January, 2020.

Not from the government, the UN, the IMF, or the African Union.

But from an entrepreneur.

The UK's first black billionaire.

This billionaire set up a $6.25 million (£4.8 million) fund which offered to pay up to 2000 hospital doctors around $300 per month for six months to give the government time to find a long-term solution.

That averted a national catastrophe and got the doctors back to work.

And saved potentially hundreds of thousands of desperate Zimbabweans from further distress.

His story starts, bizarrely, with a five-year Amber Flag Pain period with a protracted battle with this same government (well, sort of the same) with this same country on starting his business.

The fact that he was willing to pay for all the doctors in hospitals in Zimbabwe to go back to work was itself worthy of note.[95]

But that's not what made him an ideal candidate for a Pathfinder Legacy. With what he had been through with the Zimbabwean government, it's fair to say that 99.9 percent of other entrepreneurs would have turned their back on the government, never to return.

But he didn't. Even though it very nearly cost him his life.

He had had to flee the country for his life 20 years earlier from the Mugabe regime. He hadn't returned since.

In choosing a role model for the Pathfinder Legacy, we considered many billionaire entrepreneurs across the world who had built a successful business and had made a huge impact through their personal leadership example and/or philanthropic efforts.

Bill Gates, founder of Microsoft and of the Bill and Melinda Gates Foundation, endowed with close to $50 billion, which has fought poverty, disease, and inequity throughout the world for the past 20 years, would have been a prime candidate.

So would the late Vichai Srivaddhanaprabha, Thai billionaire, founder, owner, and chairman of King Power travel retail group in Thailand, who had brought much joy to the English Premier Football league through his exemplary leadership of Leicester Football Club and millions of dollars to the Vichai Srivaddhanaprabha Foundation. So much so that the Asian Awards honoured him posthumously in 2019 with the Outstanding Contribution to the Community award.

Or Richard Branson, the effervescent British billionaire, founder of the wildly successful Virgin Group, who has pledged to give away half of his $6 billion

---

95 https://deliverypdf.ssrn.com/delivery.php

fortune to charity and supports over 28 causes, 37 charities, and is the founder of Virgin Unite in 2004, where he now spends the majority of his time—building new alliances, helping entrepreneurs, supporting charitable causes, or working on conservation, drug policy, criminal justice reform, and LGBTQ+ rights.

Or the brilliant Warren Buffett, who needs no introduction.

But we kept coming back to one name.

Strive Masiyiwa.

He's not the most well-known, or richest, or loudest. He's not without controversy. But we chose him as the Pathfinder because his fortune was birthed in the desert. In the wilderness. In hopelessness. And he's redefined philanthropy from just throwing money at problems to a resolutely strategic bent. In so doing, he has created a path for over 250,000 leaders and counting—out of the desert.

He built his legacy, and fortune, and leadership through fears, tears, blood, and sweat.

Strive Masiyiwa was born in Zimbabwe (then Rhodesia) on 29 January, 1961. He left when Prime Minister Ian Smith declared independence from Britain in 1968. He settled in Kitwe, Zambia's third biggest city, and then moved to Scotland. His mother, an entrepreneur in her own right, and his father, a civil servant, were able to offer him a private education in Edinburgh. He returned to help fight the guerrilla war started by Robert Mugabe to liberate the country from white rule but was advised by a fellow freedom fighter to rather concentrate on rebuilding the country since the war had virtually been won.

He therefore went back to Britain, obtained a Bachelor's in Electrical Engineering from the University of Wales, worked for a while in Cambridge, and then returned to work for the Zimbabwe Posts and Telecommunications Corporation, (PTC). At that time, 75 percent of Zimbabweans had never heard a phone ring, let alone even owned a phone.

In 1987, he decided to start a side hustle called Retrofit, in part to build his own house. However, the company became so profitable that he was able to quit working for the PTC. Retrofit became so profitable that it gained Masiyiwa countrywide recognition, turned the eyes of the government on him, and at one point resulted in his being abducted by the country's intelligence bureau. "I thought I was a dead man," he said, recounting the experience decades later. "I prayed in the car on the way to the cell. I prayed all day in the cell. People say I am a religious man; it started on that day."

His "prayers" were heard. He came out of that meeting with a renewed sense of purpose: to let Mugabe's government understand the importance of black businesses. Mugabe met black businesses leaders, through which the Indigenous Business Development Centre (IBDC), an organisation to promote local black Zimbabwean businesses, was formed.

The IBDC benefitted Masiyiwa immensely, leading to revenues of 100 million Zimbabwean dollars at its peak, high-level security clearance, main business coming from the armed forces, and even a contract for President Mugabe's rural home.

However, that "knock" for mobile telephones still featured in his dreams:

> ...I saw the opportunity to provide a service in a way that had never been pro-
> vided before. At that time, although cellular was very much a prestige thing, the
> average African country that had even introduced cellular had an average of 5,000
> subscribers, just for the super-rich, and I believed that this was a misuse of the
> technology...at that time things like prepaid had not been developed which would
> see millions of people become subscribers. And we were one of the first people
> to introduce it in Africa. So I was very clear in my mind where I wanted to go.

So, he applied for a licence to operate a cellular network. Outrageously, the PTC rejected his request, citing lack of demand, but really, they wanted to maintain their monopoly, so in their minds, a private firm was out of the question.

So then began a five-year, costly, ding-dong legal challenge that almost rendered Masiyiwa bankrupt and went all the way to the Zimbabwe Supreme Court. His legal team, with informal help from the famous American lawyer, used highly technical arguments. It was then that he drew strength from his Christian faith to be a trailblazer, a Pathfinder in clean business:

> You know, as a born-again Christian, I took a decision daily to persuade myself to practice my convictions. And, as a businessman in that environment, there was nothing more obvious that to succeed, to do anything, it was all about patronage and corruption. I didn't see that we would have a future in African business as long as it was totally associated with corruption. If you go to the average man on the street and you ask them what they think of businesspeople, they talk of kickbacks, corruption. We didn't have an image to present to the next generation. And so I decided I wanted to make that stand.

So, he mounted a constitutional challenge to PTC's monopoly, citing Section 20 of the Zimbabwean Constitution—*every Zimbabwean has a right to receive and impart information without hindrance.* Masiyiwa was strongly advised against filing this, as it was tantamount to a rebellion against Mugabe himself. At that time, Zimbabwe had only 145,000 telephones, which translated to 1.3 telephones per 100 people. Over 95,000 were on the waiting list. Some people had to try as many as 10 times to complete a call.

Mugabe's government was furious. Masiyiwa recalled:

> The government was just absolutely livid. I mean, people told me that they had people come to tell me the things the President had said, and that the generals had said, and… the whole system turned on me, the Secret Service, everything. Retrofit lost all its government work, as well as not being paid for all the work we had done to date. We were just ordered to leave government sites, everything.

Masiyiwa's family, friends, associates, and colleagues started receiving physical and death threats. Zimbabweans frequently got held in prison on Fridays and then released on Mondays to try to break his spirit. But he was always able to escape arrest, even to the point of hiding in the boot of his friend's car. His phones were tapped. He was followed everywhere by plainclothes policemen, so he frequently spent the weekend in hiding.

And to top it all, the government was also attempting to take over white-owned businesses, which Masiyiwa was against, and conversely his black colleagues were for, so he resigned from the leadership of the IBDC, which caused even more controversy.

And on top that, as if to rub insult to injury, he even hired Marion Moore, a white Zimbabwean, who was also a woman, to be his Chief Financial Officer in November 1995. But Strive didn't hire her because she was white. Or a woman. He hired her because in an era of lack of talent, she was competent professionally, had professional accounting qualifications, and had worked for several years in the IT industry. But for Strive Masiyiwa, that was not enough. She also had a crucial element that was scarce in those days.

Character.

She was surprised about the number of personal questions he asked her about her family at the interview before he hired her.

Recalling the experience, she said:

> It was the most amazing company to work in. I learnt about the resilience of willpower and leadership. And in those years, Strive—and I think that was one of the things—he's on a huge pedestal for me, he's sort of one of my heroes—and in that time, his own dedication and his own—he did it selflessly because when—I mean, we ran on no money. That was another revelation to me, that you can operate with very little money, and with the will, anything can be achieved.

But he was prepared to pay the price to maintain a clean, ethical business.

After a while, he realised he couldn't save Retrofit, so he sold it to the CEO of its biggest supplier, who eagerly bought it off him. Masiyiwa then went all in and gave birth to his new venture, Enhanced Telecommunications Network (Econet).

But the battle was not over, not by a long shot.

Now that Econet Wireless had become a business, the PTC had now realised the potential in mobile telephones, so it entered the fray by setting up its own mobile service—at the time there were only two slots available, so it took over the other slot as well and tried to get Ericsson-made equipment. Masiyiwa took out a court injunction against its use, seeing it as a plot by Mugabe to kill Econet's battle for a licence.

Surprisingly, the Supreme Court ruled against the PTC in August 1995, stating that a monopoly violated Zimbabwe's constitution, and that it would take almost 15 years for the PTC to clear the 95,000 backlog at its current expansion rate, and gave Econet permission to build a network.

Masiyiwa then entered into negotiations with Ericsson and Mo Ibrahim's Celtell, offering them stakes in the business.

But Mugabe, being Mugabe, had one final roar left in him.

He was planning to issue a presidential decree against Econet, which would overturn the Supreme Court verdict and reset the clock to zero. Masiyiwa's brilliant lawyer suggested that if Econet could install some equipment and commence transmission before the decree was issued, it could claim what is termed grandparenting rights—a clause or statute which permits the operator of a business to be exempt from restrictions on use if the business continues to be used as it was when the law was adopted.

So Masiyiwa quickly installed some base stations, advertised in local newspapers, and set it up as an alternative mobile business. The public responded, and over 5,000 subscribers applied.

On 5ᵗʰ Feb, 1996, President Mugabe finally issued the decree and explained to *Newsweek* that he wasn't out to floor Masiyiwa, but to ensure other interested parties had a chance to get a phone licence.

Masiyiwa responded when asked about this with the now-famous statement: *"I don't pay bribes."*

It got ugly.

Celltel reneged on its agreement with Econet, asked for its money back, and proceeded to set up its own company—helped in part by recruiting new partners, including the president's nephew, some ministers, and other VIPs.

But help was to come from an unexpected source. An almost miraculous source.

After Celltel was awarded the license, an American missionary walked into Masiyiwa's office and demanded an Econet line. Despite Masiyiwa's insistence that he couldn't have one, the missionary insisted on prepaying immediately for a line, offering 10,000 Zimbabwean dollars (around $3,000 then). The missionary also lined up several candidates who would become customers. Then the international media got involved, then local students of the University of Zimbabwe, then ordinary citizens.

Econet presented a 100-page letter to the Zimbabwe Government Tender Board outlining its reasoning to the objection to the licence given to Celltel. The GTB wrote to the government to instruct Celltel to stop operations whilst these were being investigated, but the Information Minister, who turned out to be a referee to Celltel, rejected it.

The GTB prevailed, even without the need for a judge, and Celltel was ordered to stop operating, and finally, in July 1998, the license was signed for Econet to begin formal operations in Zimbabwe.

In May 2000, Masiyiwa had to flee the country to South Africa, where he founded Econet Wireless, a brand new and completely different entity than the one in Zimbabwe.

But the battle that reared its head was repeated in Nigeria, where Econet lost $300 million because Masiyiwa refused to pay close to $4 million in bribes. But with his characteristic nerves of steel, he sued the officials concerned, got them in prison, recovered his money, and Econet Nigeria (now Airtel) is one of the most dynamic mobile companies in the sub-continent of West Africa.

And in Kenya, where his licence was cancelled in 2004, the company was even labelled as a fraud with no place in the country. But he wore the government down and was finally granted a licence. The company counted 200,000 subscribers just a couple of years later.

He stood by his ethics, paid the price, and reaped the rewards. Largely because of his battles, 88 percent of Zimbabweans now own a mobile phone according to Statista (2020).

He has inverted the pyramid.

I don't pay bribes.

From its humble beginnings in Zimbabwe in 1997, Econet Global now has business operations in over 20 countries in Africa, Latin America, the UAE, and China. Econet Zimbabwe is the second biggest company by market capitalisation in Zimbabwe. His Liquid Telecom group is Africa's largest satellite and fibre optic business, which spans over 14 countries. Econet Wireless have significant shares in market-leading telecoms Rwanda Telecom, Lesotho Telecom, Econet Wireless South Africa, Solarway, and Transaction Processing Systems (TPS).

He also founded Cassava Technologies, which operates Liquid Intelligent Technologies. Liquid owns and operates Africa's largest cross-border fibre optic network spanning over 100,000 km from Cape Town to Cairo, Port Sudan to Lagos, and Dar Es Salaam to the West Coast of Congo and covers more than 300 towns and cities across Africa.

Cassava Technologies also operates Africa's largest network of carrier-neutral, state-of-the-art interconnected data centres and cloud-based technology that supports Africa's participation in the global digital economy.

He also partnered with one of America's leading entrepreneurs to build New Zealand's third mobile network, 2degrees. He owns multi-million-dollar estates in New York, London, and South Africa, valued at over $50 million.

He paid the price to be an ethical entrepreneur, and today, the results speak for themselves.

This is not to say he didn't make missteps or was never embroiled in controversy. He was rebuked by a leading theologian in Zimbabwe for claiming 'messianic status' in how he used the Bible for inspiration.

His wife, Tsitsi, and Strive himself were forced to delete their Twitter Accounts in 2019, and she was forced to apologise when she implied Zimbabweans were lazy and that they had no sense of urgency and desperation with their work ethic.[96]

But his motivations have never been in doubt.

It took almost two decades, but now he is the UK's first black billionaire. The first African and only black person to sit on the board of Netflix. He is also on the board of Unilever, the Bill and Melinda Gates Foundation, the Rockefeller Foundation, and the National Geographic Society. He is the only African on the US Holocaust Memorial Museum's Committee on Conscience and is on the Global Advisory Boards of Bank of America,

---

96 https://www.techzim.co.zw/2019/01/tsitsi-and-strive-masiyiwa-delete-twitter-accounts-strive-says-tsitsi-was-being-cyber-bullied/

the Council of Foreign Relations, Stanford University, and the Prince of Wales Trust for Africa.

And the accolades continue to follow.

He has been named by Fortune as one of the World's 50 Greatest Leaders in May 2021 and, in December 2020, was named by Bloomberg as one of the world's 50 most influential people. *Fortune Magazine* named him on the list of the World's 50 Greatest Leaders, and the *New African* magazine names him as one of the 100 most influential Africans for 2020, and the International Rescue Committee awarded him the Freedom Award. Some media houses go as far to say that he is projected to be the richest African by 2030.

But his achievements don't stop there.

We've already spoke about his achievements for COVID for Africa at the beginning of this book.

He has organised 250,000 scholarships for African students, as well as 40,000 orphans, through his philanthropic arm, the Higher Life Foundation, which he founded with his wife Tsitsi Masiyiwa.

In an interview for the African Philanthropy Forum, he stated that philanthropy is not giving away money. It is not charity and gifting aid.

It consists in addressing needs in a strategic, methodical way. For Masiyiwa, philanthropy is a generational undertaking which emphasises education. It reminds me of Stephen Covey's bestselling book, *Principle-Centered Leadership*, which has as its central theme, "Give a man a fish and you feed him for a day; teach him to fish and feed him for a lifetime."[97]

At the closing stages of that interview, he stated:

---

97 Covey, Stephen. Principle-Centred Leadership (New York, Summit Books 1990)

If you really want a legacy, if you want to lay down the foundations for people to remember you for the right reasons, then philanthropy is the way to go. Not knee-jerk reactions to give away money, but real systematic areas—identifying strategically what you're good at and working with others to push that through.[98]

Working with others?

He is a cofounder with Richard Branson of the Carbon War Room and the B-Team. A co-founder with the late Kofi Annan, UN Secretary General, and the Bill and Melinda Gates Foundation for the Alliance for a Green Revolution in Africa, an initiative to help 400 million African small-holder farms, he now serves as its Chairman Emeritus and was honoured for this work with the Norman Borlaug World Food Prize Medallion.

And in March 2022, his wife, Tsitsi, and other world philanthropists came together to raise $1 billion to advance gender equality and women's leadership.

As she said in an interview with *Forbes*, "The need is so great. The need is now. The need is massive, and to not do anything is doing a huge disservice to the next generation. We owe it to the next generation."[99]

That is the Pathfinder Legacy.

A Power Legacy through personal philanthropy.

There are almost 300,000 Africans and counting who have been educated through philanthropy, as well as millions of farmers who have been helped to start their own farms, multiplying prosperity throughout the continent.

But not only that.

---

98 Why Give: Strive Masiyiwa, Founder, Higher Life Foundation – Interview with the African Philanthopy Forum, (APF) assessed 11 Feb 2022 https://www.youtube.com/watch?v=xkfZXZP8s58
99 https://www.forbesafrica.com/frontrunner/2022/05/04/the-need-is-so-greattsitsi-masiyiwa-on-new-gender-fund/

He has extended his philanthropy by inverting the pyramid. He also sponsors successful American graduates to take up jobs in Africa's leading companies. This has also been an extremely successful venture—the Americans and Europeans who take up these offers find themselves pleasantly surprised, and most, more often than not, do not want to return to their native countries. In doing so, he has contributed in demystifying Africa as an exotic continent where people go to watch climbing gorillas and running lions and hyenas, to countries where people can actually do business.

And a Place Legacy though a successful business. Not just a successful business, but in market-creating innovations.

In their book *The Prosperity Paradox*, the renowned late Professor Cristensen and his co-authors Nigerian Efoso Ojomo and Karen Dillon state:

In the struggle lies opportunity:

Market-creating innovations do exactly what the name implies—they create new markets. But not just any markets, new markets that serve people for whom either no markets existed, or existing products were neither affordable nor accessible for a variety of reasons. These innovations transform complicated and expensive products into ones that are so much more affordable and accessible that many more people are able to buy and use them....in a sense, market-creating innovations democratise previously exclusive products and services.

They continue:

This type of innovation not only create markets, but jobs, too. This is because as new markets with new consumers are born, companies must hire more people to market, distribute, sell and service the product. Market-creating innovations have the potential to create what we call local and global jobs.[100]

---

100 Christensen, Ojomo and Dillon: The Prosperity Paradox (2019 Harper Business, New York)

Today, Econet Zimbabwe is the second-biggest company in the country by way of market capitalisation, employs over 2,000 direct employees, and has over 12 million connected customers, not to mention the hundreds of thousands of cottage industries that have sprung up that employ millions of other Zimbabweans, entrepreneurs, and other employees. This is not to mention the millions of other jobs that have been created through breakthrough industries that rely on the telecommunications networks Econet has built throughout the continent and beyond.

So in innovating, he has also created prosperity for millions of Africans.

Not bad for a company starred originally with just $75.

So in the Pathfinder Legacy, the Power and Place Legacies synergise each other to create a positive, explosive legacy.

This brings us full circle.

Literally.

Because as I wrote the final sentences of this book, as I prepared to send this book to the publishers in a weird sort of way, this book ended as it started.

The same triggers.

The very next morning, as I came back from the gym with Dela, I was in the bath, and everything went black. I had passed out from another massive epileptic fit.

As I came to, I had fallen out of the bath, on the floor, stark naked, wet and helpless, and, as always, Dela was right there to rescue me from potential life-changing and permanent harm. I owe a lot to that woman.

The same thing happened again at work that very same day three hours later.

I had passed out on the floor, twitching—they nearly called the ambulance, but I came to, just in time.

I owe a lot to those employees and partners.

I hurriedly took an entire day off to finish the book and send it off. Who knows? It could be my last.

So, another appointment to the neurologist, another potential change in medication, another lesson in humility, and another lesson in the importance of legacy.

A reinforcement of the fragility of life, the Church of Scars. Nothing teaches us humility and brings things home quite like pain, especially White Flag Pain and Red Flag Pain.

And the importance of leaving a Pathfinder Legacy, every day, every moment, for the rest of your life on this blessed and weird home we call Earth.

And to repeat what author Ben Horowitz says in his 2019 book, *What You Do Is Who You Are,*

> Keep death in mind at all times like a samurai. It's good for business. Keep that in mind, and if you do die today, or if your business folds, you can still look back on it with pride… as a samurai would.

To quote again from Adam Grant:

> *The ultimate test of success is not whether you're proud of what you have achieved. It's whether you're proud of who you've become. Accomplishments highlight your skills. Relationships highlight your values. If excellence is what you do, then character is what you do for others.*

So who is a Pathfinder?

A Pathfinder = Excellence + Character.

The real definition of success, and the raison d'être for this book.

Wise words for the ethical entrepreneur. Begin your business with this end in mind, and you will have fulfilled the raison d'être for this book.

KEY CONCEPTS:
- The Philanthropist
- The Purist
- The Profligate
- The Pathfinder

QUESTIONS
1. What kind of legacy do you want to leave? Describe it as vividly and with as much detail as you can.

2. Did the legacy you describe in the previous question amount to that of a Pathfinder?

3. The Pathfinder is held aloft as the highest form of legacy. Are there any obstacles which prevent you from becoming a Pathfinder?

EPILOGUE

Hello, I'm Abhinav, cofounder and partner (with Steven) of Emerald Management Group. We've been partners for a decade and been through some hair-raising moments together.

At the outset, I would like to congratulate Steven for accomplishing one of the most daunting challenges he's faced in his long and storied career so far—authoring a book. When he first brought up the idea many moons back, I, well and truly and justifiably so, believed that he was kidding. Writing a book is no easy task, specially for someone like Steven who is a serial entrepreneur with projects across the world. My first question was, "How would you even take out time to write something?" But take out the time he did, and over the next many months, he put his head down and met every deadline he set for himself, which is quite unlike him, to be honest. I know this for a fact, since he regularly spammed me with chapters to review!

Anyway, Steven and I go back many years. We were together in a couple of modules in the Warwick MBA program and managed to keep in touch, despite both of us having busy and erratic schedules. Being a Management Consultant with The Strategy Boutique and Emerald Group and working across the world, we are constantly on the lookout for new projects and opportunities to grow and scale up our business. And when our first opportunity to work together came up, we immediately grabbed it with both hands. It started off at a hotel near Heathrow, where we discussed the nuances of the project and immediately hit the ground running. No paperwork, no contracts (not then, in any case). That's the person Steven is—he is loyal, believes in people, and works extremely hard to accomplish what he sets out to do. And above all, he's a great friend, and colleague.

To say our journey has been all rosy would be facetious. We have had our ups and downs over the last 10 years, problems compounded by the fact that Africa is one of the hardest places in the world to do business in. But Steven's steadfastness towards making a difference there has been what's kept him and our association going, not just in Africa, but in many other places where we work. We have had our fair share of fallouts and disagreements over the course of this journey, despite our differences—race, age, background, training—but the fact that we both stand for the same core principles (Fairness, Integrity, Accountability and Transparency) has ensured a very high level of mutual respect.

Lastly, it would be a tad unfair if I didn't weigh in (briefly) on the book. As I mentioned earlier, I have seen this book evolve, page by page, chapter by chapter, and I think the final product is an extremely compelling read. It has surpassed my already high expectations from the book, and I would urge everyone to get their copies as soon as they can. The Spotify playlist lends a unique, personal, and relatable perspective to some of his real-life stories and experiences, and I'm sure you'll agree that it adds another dimension to what is already an excellent literary work.

Steven, it has been a privilege working with you, something that all my colleagues who have worked with you would attest to, and here's to more great work together. To the next decade and beyond!

- Abhinav Srivastava
Partner - The Strategy Boutique and Emerald Group
Dubai, UAE

ACKNOWLEDGEMENTS

This book has taken a truly superhuman effort, almost literally, of an army of human angelic beings, true ethical people in every sense of the word, and I can never thank these people enough. To avoid duplication, and to stick to the number of words I've been allotted, I'll try to be as brief as I can and not mention again those heroes I have already mentioned in the actual book. If I've missed you out for any reason, I take full responsibility. I'm still a diamond in the rough. I'm working at being more organised without quashing my creative self—my vice verses—a very tall ask!

My beautiful, forgiving, and wise wife, Dela, who endured the endless morning tap…tap…tap and talking… and questions and who served as my sounding board for these concepts.

My son Nana, who helped me refine the scientific concepts—Rutherford and the Periodic Table—and adapted them for this.

I said I wouldn't duplicate, but I make an exception for Nshira, my daughter. Her support has been indescribable, incredible, hard to put into words—this book would not be a reality without her. Simple.

The same goes to Sir Professor Myles Wickstead. This book would be nonexistent if you hadn't called me on that Monday morning, Myles. Thank you for all your support. And for writing such a beautiful foreword. I am forever in your debt.

A very special mention to Hasan Kubba, coauthor of 2021's U.K. Best Business Book, *The Unfair Advantage*. We had a conference call right at the beginning of my writing. Your humility and advice were inspirational and served as a guiding light throughout this book. Your friendship and mentorship have been exceptional. Thank you for opening the door and keeping it open for us.

My childhood friend Emmanuel Apea. Thank you for your support over the last 40 years. I don't take it for granted.

My parents, who live 6,000 miles away, Nana and Rose, and my extended family in Ghana.

My beta readers; Jeremiah Amegashie, Catherine Hutchins, Consultant Nick Shuff, Frances Hallett, Dr. Moji Olugbode, Brian Martin, Michael Adjei, Bernice Atubra, Akofa Wallace. Thank you for all your invaluable suggestions. I hope I've done you proud.

Melanie Butler, Waterstones staff member, thank you for believing my book was good enough to get into the U.K.'s biggest bookstore chain, Waterstones. You switched the light on. Thank you. You are a credit to your employers.

And all the celebrities who took the time to read through the rough manuscript to endorse this book, Professor Elikem Kuenyehia, Charlie Robertson, Charlotte Osei, Christian Stadler, Anderson Hirst, Claire Oatway, Ernest Darkoh, Robert Smith, Les Funtleyder, Sam Black, and Nick Shuff. Your belief made me believe.

And those artists and poets who helped me in those dark days without even knowing it: Yrsa Daley-Ward, Kayo Chingonyi, Caleb Femi. Your talent knows no bounds.

And the incredible Paper Raven Team! Morgan, Brian, Gabrielle, Amanda, Karen, Stef, M.A. Hinkle. I am immensely proud that this book was published by an almost all-woman team (with the notable exception of Brian, of course). You folks are phenomenal. Honestly. I'm so happy I found you. You're the best. And I'll be back.

And finally the source of my ethical bent: My unshakable Christian faith. And to the three people that have taught me the intersection of reasoned Christian enlightenment and ethical business writing and living: Reverend Geoff Lee, Carey Nieuwhof, and Pastor Mensa Otabil. I owe you a ton.

ABOUT THE AUTHOR

STEVEN N. ADJEI

Steven N. Adjei is a British-Ghanaian author, poet, award-winning pharmacist, and entrepreneur. As the founding partner of BlueCloud Health, part of the Emerald Management Group, an advisory and consulting firm with offices in London, Dubai and Delhi, he works with clients across the world.

He loves running and resides in Plymouth, a beautiful seaside city in Devon, England, with his wife Dela and two teenage children.

Steven holds an MBA from Warwick Business School and is also an executive contributor for *Brainz Magazine*. *Pay The Price* is his first book.

www.stevenadjei.com

Email: hello@stevenadjei.com

LinkedIn: Steven N. Adjei

Twitter: @stevenadjei

Instagram: stevennadjei

Facebook: stevenadjei

APPENDIX
FURTHER READING

My second book, *In Search of Permanence*, due in 2023, will go more into detail of the Formative Phase I wrote about here in *Pay The Price*.

But in the meantime… I have read literally hundreds of books on leadership, business, strategy, and entrepreneurship. These are 15 of my best, in my humble opinion:

1. Cloud Henry. Integrity: The Courage to Meet the Demands of Reality, How Six Essential Qualities Determine Your Success in Business (New York, Harper Collins, 2006)

2. Horowitz, Ben. The Hard Thing About Hard Things: Building a Business Where There Are No Hard Answers (New York, Harper Collins, 2014)

3. Cohen, Ronald. Impact: Reshaping Capitalism to Drive Real Change (London, Penguin Random House, 2020)

4. Christensen, Ojomo and Dillon. The Prosperity Paradox: How Innovation Can Lift Nations Out of Poverty (New York Harper Collins, 2020)

5. Raz, Guy. How I Built This: The Unexpected Paths to Success From the World's Most Inspiring Entrepreneurs (London, Macmillan, 2020)

6. Covey, Stephen. Principle-Centered Leadership (New York, Summit Books, 1990)

7. Mazzeo, Michael et al. Roadside MBA: Back Road Lessons for Entrepreneurs, Executives and Small Business Owners (New York Hachette Book Group, 2014)

8. Ries, Eric. The Lean Startup: How Constant Innovation Creates Radically Successful Businesses (London, Penguin 2011)

9. Greber, Michael, E. The E-Myth Revisited: Why Most Small Businesses Don't Work and What to Do About It (New York, Harper Collins, 1995)

10. Rosenzweig, Phil. The Halo Effect…and Eight Other Business Delusions That Deceive Managers (New York, Free Press, 2007)

11. Nieuwhof, Carey. Didn't See it Coming: Overcoming the 7 Greatest Challenges That No One Expects and Everyone Experiences (New York, Waterbrook, 2018)

12. Daley-Ward Yrsa. Bone (London 2014, Penguin)

13. Goldsmith, Marshall. The Earned Life (Dublin, Penguin Random House, 2022)

14. Hayman and Giles. Mission: How the Best in Business Break Through (London Penguin Random House UK 2015)

15. Grant, Adam. Give and Take: A Revolutionary Approach to Success (London, Orion Books, 2013)

Ingram Content Group UK Ltd.
Milton Keynes UK
UKHW021305110523
421589UK00024B/907